ACQUISITION OF READING SKILLS

Cultural Constraints and Cognitive Universals

ACQUISITION OF READING SKILLS

Cultural Constraints and Cognitive Universals

Edited by

BARBARA R. FOORMAN
ALEXANDER W. SIEGEL

University of Houston

LEA LAWRENCE ERLBAUM ASSOCIATES, PUBLISHERS
1986   Hillsdale, New Jersey   London

Lawrence Erlbaum Associates, Inc., Publishers
365 Broadway
Hillsdale, New Jersey 07642

Library of Congress Cataloging-in-Publication Data
Main entry under title:

Acquisition of reading skills.

Bibliography: p.
Includes index.
1. Reading — Addresses, essays, lectures. 2. Reading —
Code emphasis approaches — Addresses, essays, lectures.
3. Japanese language — Study and teaching (Elementary) —
Addresses, essays, lectures. 4. Chinese language — Study
and teaching (Elementary) — Addresses, essays, lectures.
5. English language — Study and teaching (Elementary) —
Addresses, essays, lectures. I. Foorman, Barbara R.
II. Siegel, Alexander W.
LB1050.A24 1986   372.4   85-27407
ISBN 0-89859-624-4

Contents

Preface

This book is the result of a conference, "Learning to Read: Cognitive Universals and Cultural Constraints," at the University of Houston – University Park Campus on April 18–19, 1984. The original idea for the conference came from the senior editor's contact at Oxford University during the Trinity Terms of 1981 and 1983 with Peter Bryant and Lynette Bradley. Bryant and Bradley's investigation of young children's auditory categorization skills suggested that experiences children have with rhyme and alliteration underlie these skills. Foorman was intrigued with the possibility of rhyme and alliteration as precursors to learning to read, but she questioned the universality of these poetic activities. For example, *haiku* and *waku* poetry in Japanese are based on the number of syllables, not on intrasyllabic relationships that are found in English poetry. So the conference was called to bring together Bryant's thesis with appropriate commentators to discuss, in concrete ways, cognitive universals and cultural constraints in learning to read. Did the Japanese linguistic and cultural context suppress the role of rhyme and alliteration, or indeed were these poetic activities not universal at all?

We invited Giyoo Hatano from Dokkyo University in Tokyo and Harold Stevenson from the University of Michigan and the Bush Program in Child Development and Social Policy to offer their insights concerning cultural constraints involved in learning to read. Professor Hatano is a cognitive psychologist well known for his experiments on the reading process in Japanese and his interest in early childhood education. Harold Stevenson has expanded experimental child psychology with his cross-cultural research and his commitment to public policy. Professor Stevenson's study of the Japanese language while he was in the United States Navy and his recent cross-cultural investigation of reading and math achievement in Japan, the United States, and Taiwan made him a logical conference participant.

We invited Charles Perfetti from the University of Pittsburgh and the Learning Research and Development Center to complement Professor Bryant on the "universal" side of the discussion. Professor Perfetti's verbal efficiency theory gave us a cognitive science model of reading to compare with other participants' models of reading and evidence of cultural constraints.

Discussants are on the faculty at the University of Houston – University Park. Because of her extensive research on children's acquisition and retention of verbal material, we asked Professor Elizabeth Ghatala to comment on Charles Perfetti's discussion. Alex Siegel, whose research exemplifies a similar interest in contextual perspectives in cognitive development, was a natural choice to discuss Harold Stevenson's paper. As a developmental psycholinguist with some familiarity with Japanese language and culture, Barbara Foorman reviews Giyoo Hatano's paper. In the last four years, Professor Foorman has done comparative experimental research on language and cognitive development in Japan and the United States with the help of Professor Hatano's colleagues at Hokkaido, Saitama, and Miyazaki Universities. And, finally, Jerome Rosner from the University of Houston's College of Optometry was asked to comment on Peter Bryant's work because of the Auditory Analysis Test he developed with Dorothea Simon while at the University of Pittsburgh's Learning Research Development Center. Professor Rosner's experience with assessing and training young children's skills in deleting sounds from words provides a clinical perspective on the issue of phonological awareness.

In addition to thanking our conference participants, we would like to acknowledge the financial support provided by the University of Houston, Center for Public Policy (part of the College of Social Sciences), the College of Optometry, and the Office of the Provost. We would also like to extend our gratitude to Denise Boyd for doing the index, to Tessa Jo Smith and Haruko Oda for their help in preparing the manuscript, and to Mary Alice Doyle, Judy Feigin, and Nancy Hightower for their help in organizing the conference.

Barbara R. Foorman
Alexander Siegel
Houston, Texas

Introduction

Barbara R. Foorman
University of Houston

In literate societies around the world, children begin instruction in reading somewhere between the ages of five and seven years. On one level, their tasks are very similar — learn the sound-symbol relationships of their languages and apply their linguistic and cognitive skills to gain meaning from print. On another level their tasks seem to vary — orthographies and sound–symbol relationships differ, and cultures' attitudes towards reading and children's motivation to achieve range widely.

This book looks at both universal and culturally constrained aspects of the process of learning to read. The first four chapters — Perfetti, Ghatala, Bryant, and Rosner — exemplify cognitive universal approaches to reading; the last four — Hatano, Foorman, Stevenson, and Siegel — highlight cultural constraints.

In Chapter 1 Perfetti presents his verbal efficiency model of reading. For Perfetti reading is the ability to gain understanding from print, with decoding an important aspect of this ability. There are three major component processes in his model of reading: lexical access, propositional encoding, and text modeling. Lexical access leads to all the information stored in memory about a word — "the semantic encoding of the conceptual features along with the name code" (pp. 20–21, Ch. 1). Because lexical access triggers propositional encoding which, in turn, affects and is affected by text modeling, the central role played by lexical access is clear in his interactive model of reading. For Perfetti the difference between low and high ability readers is that the former spend a lot of effort on lexical processing and propositional encoding whereas the latter are able to focus on text modeling. To become a skilled reader, one must apply cognitive and linguistic components of word

knowledge within adequate working memory. Perfetti takes a representa-
tional approach to word knowledge, in contrast to Laberge and Samuels'
(1974) automaticity approach. Rather than focusing on developing more active letter–word links, Perfetti's approach centers on the quality of representation nodes. Perfetti stresses that quality is enhanced by the redundancy of
the representation system, where words have graphemic and phonetic representations and are composed of letters, orthographic patterns, and
phonemes.

Are there cultural constraints on Verbal Efficiency Theory? Perfetti re-
gards verbal efficiency as a quasi-universal in that the hypothesis that comprehension takes place within the limits posed by lexical processes is likely to
be true of nonalphabetic codes as well as alphabetic. The development of lexical ability is also probably quasi-universal. Constraints imposed on lexical
access by the symbol system and general language ability appear to be universal. However, the relationship between symbols and sounds varies in alphabetic, syllabary, and logographic systems. Consequently, the lexical representation system is the least likely candidate for universality. But, Perfetti
suggests, the "architecture" of the representation system may be fairly
general.

In Chapter 2 Elizabeth Ghatala comments on Verbal Efficiency Theory
and points to the need to support the link between decoding and comprehension. She discusses in detail a study by Palincsar and Brown (1984), who
found that training in comprehension strategies and monitoring improved
comprehension of seventh grade poor readers yet did not improve decoding.
Such a finding does not negate Verbal Efficiency Theory's emphasis on
decoding fluency, Ghatala mentions, but does underscore the need for training studies designed to test the causal role of decoding. She cites one such
study by Frederiksen and others (Frederiksen, Weaver, Waren, Gillotte,
Roseberry, Freeman, & Goodman, 1983), in which ten secondary students
low in reading skills played computer games designed to improve lexical accessibility. There were impressive gains when skills were hierarchically sequenced, but evidence of transfer to comprehension was less strong.

Peter Bryant's approach to reading in Chapter 3 is also within a cognitive
universals framework but differs in important ways from Perfetti and
Ghatala's positions. Bryant harnesses two traditional methods of developmental psychology in his study of causal factors in learning to read — the longitudinal approach and the training study — and insists on a Reading Age
Match (RAM) rather than a Mental Age Match (MAM) design. Longitudinal
studies can establish relationships that occur naturally but may not be causal.
Just the opposite is true of training studies: causal relationships may be established that are artifacts of the experiment. Thus, through study of a problem
longitudinally as well as with training, genuine, causal relationships may be
established.

To study reading problems, Bryant suggests coupling the longitudinal-training approach with matching children on the basis of reading level rather than mental age. The danger of matching good and poor readers on the basis of mental age — say, 10 years of age for good and poor readers of average intelligence — is that the process of learning to read may be the *cause*, not the effect, of performance differences in reading. Bryant points out that memory for words and speed of word production are two assumed causes of reading differences that may well be the *result* of learning to read. To disentangle cause and effect in these areas, one should match children on reading ability. Then, when differences do occur between, say, 8-year-olds and 10-year-olds of the same reading ability, one can be more assured that the area under investigation is the cause of the older children's reading problems.

Bradley and Bryant (1983) have applied the longitudinal training approach to the study of phonological skills. They showed that the phonological skills of rhyming and alliteration predicted reading and spelling (in contrast to math), independent of intelligence, over four years. They also showed that training poor readers in rhyme and alliteration skills versus conceptual categorization skills improved reading but not math performance. Thus, their work is convincing in establishing a causal connection between rhyming and alliteration skill and reading success. But is this skill universal? Bryant implies that rhyme and alliteration universally require categorization of words on the basis of common sounds. Such categorization requires attention to constituent sounds in much the same way that the alphabet does and that Japanese kana (in contrast to kanji) does. Bryant's evidence for phonological awareness in reading kana comes from a study (Kimura & Bryant, 1983) in which Japanese and English children read and wrote words with and without concurrent vocalization. Concurrent vocalization did not interfere with reading and writing kanji or reading English words, but it did interfere with reading and writing kana words and writing English. Kimura and Bryant concluded that spelling English words, in contrast to reading English words, demands application of sound-symbol relationships. In the Japanese scripts it is the reading and writing of kana rather than kanji that demand prelexical phonological analysis. I currently have a student, Mi Hyun Cho, who is replicating the Kimura and Bryant study with Korean children. Korean utilizes an alphabet (Hangul) and Chinese characters (Hanja). By investigating the effects of auditory and visual interference on first graders' reading and writing of Hangul and Hanji, we can examine *within* a culture the relative contributions of phonological versus visual analysis in alphabetic and logographic scripts.

Bryant's points about the role of phonological analysis within and across languages and cultures are further examined in the chapters by Rosner and Hatano. Rosner agrees that auditory analysis skills play a casual role in learning to read. He claims that this causal relationship appears to be connected directly to decoding and only indirectly to comprehension, whereas visual analysis skills are linked directly to reading comprehension and are independent of decoding. For Rosner, auditory analysis skills are operationally exemplified in the ability to delete the initial consonant sound from a spoken word. Bryant feels that such sound deletion tasks, as well as syllable-tapping tasks, are more difficult than rhyming and alliteration tasks, which require a response to only part of a word. For example, Bryant's task requires that the odd word be identified in such groupings as *fun, pin, bun, gun,* and *bus, bun, rug.* Sound deletion tasks such as Rosner's provide a word and then ask that the work be repeated without a syllable or without a consonant. For example, "Say *cowboy* . . . now say it again, but leave off *cow.*" Or, "Say *spark* . . . now say it again, but don't say /p/." Bryant suggests that operating on one sound in one position, as his oddity task demands, may precede reading, while attending to all sounds is something a child must do while learning how to read.

The causal link between phonological awareness and reading acquisition has been well established (Bradley & Bryant, 1983; Perfetti, Beck, & Hughes, 1981; Treiman & Baron, 1983; Williams, 1980). Two questions come to mind. First, is phonological awareness a general cognitive and general linguistic ability that overrides differences in kinds of tasks, task instructions, and location of phonological contrast? Second, is phonological awareness a meaningful construct across languages and cultures? Recent research by Stanovich, Cunningham, and Cramer (1984) suggests that the answer to the first question is yes. They administered ten different phonological tasks to a group of kindergarten children and then assessed their reading achievement one year later. The ten tasks represented fairly well the phonological task domain described by Lewkowicz (1980) (e.g., word-to-word matching, rhyme recognition, phoneme deletion, phoneme substitution, and identification of missing phoneme). The ten tasks were: rhyme supply, rhyme choice, initial consonant same, final consonant same, strip initial consonant, substitute initial consonant, initial consonant not same, final consonant different, initial consonant different, and supply initial consonant. The rhyme supply, rhyme choice, and substitute initial consonant tasks were rhyming tasks, with the first two explicitly using the word "rhyme" in the task instructions and the third essentially requiring the child to produce a rhyme (i.e., "If I say the word *go,* and then change the first sound by changing it to /n/, what will the new word be?"). The strip initial consonant task was adapted from Bruce (1964) and Calfee, Chapman, and Venezky (1972) and is similar to Rosner's task (Rosner & Simon, 1971) described earlier. The supply initial consonant task provides a pair of words that are the same except for the initial phoneme (e.g., *cat* and *at*). The child is asked to say the sound in the first word that is missing in the second. The other five tasks are alliteration or final consonant tasks where instructions vary in the use of "same," "not same," and "different."

Stanovich et al. (1984) found a ceiling effect for the three rhyming tasks. The other seven tasks were all moderately correlated with reading ability and, as a set, were all predictive of first grade reading achievement — more predictive than IQ or a reading readiness test. Moreover, factor analysis revealed the phonological tasks to load on one factor. These results support the validity of the phonological awareness construct as awareness of the constituent sounds in words — awareness crucial to success in beginning reading. The hierarchical ordering of these ten tasks, with rhyming being easiest and deletion most difficult, also supports Bryant's point about skills necessary for learning to read versus skills acquired as a result of learning how to read. Bryant (personal communication, April 18, 1984) has suggested that the crucial link between these skills may be the ability to categorize words on the basis of common sounds in *different* positions. For example, instead of finding the odd word among *pip, pin, hill, pig,* the child might be asked to name the word which does *not* have the same sound as the other two words in *bug, tip, pon.* The ability to see that *tip* and *pon* share a common /p/ sound and that *bug* does not share this sound is an important step in realizing the alphabetic principle. One of my students, Nancy Hightower, is currently training kindergartners in multiposition sound categorization and Bradley and Bryant's (1983) rhyme and alliteration categorization to see if reading achievement can be improved.

Having examined evidence for postulating the construct of phonological awareness, consider the issue of its generalizability — particularly its generalizability across cultures and languages. In Giyoo Hatano's chapter we learn of the absence of rhyme in Japanese. Yet Japanese children engage in word play that might be just as essential to grasping the nature of the Japanese syllabary (kana) as rhyme appears to be for the English alphabet. Hatano sees phonological awareness as important to the acquisition of children's Japanese orthography (CJO) because children must be able to separate the first sound from the rest of a word in order to see its relationship to the kana symbol. Japanese children are exposed to the sound-symbol correspondence for the basic 48 kana through blocks, each depicting a picture and the initial kana of the word representing that picture. English-speaking children learn the sounds of the letters of the alphabet with similarly constructed alphabet cards. The difference is that English-speaking children also have to learn the letter names of the alphabet. Perhaps rhyme and alliteration continue to be part of reading readiness because they provide overlearned patterns for categorizing sounds that reduce memory demands for the beginning reader. In the many-to-one environment of mapping sounds to letters, the young reader of English needs regularity.

We learn from Hatano that learning to read Japanese is no easy matter. What the Japanese children gain initially by the one-to-one mapping of sound to basic kana, they lose as they have to blend sounds in order to read the special syllables. Although children quickly learn to "read" stories written in kana because they can pronounce all the words, their comprehension lags behind. Hatano attributes the lag to slow retrieval of sounds and to attentional demands of special syllables. Starting in first grade, Japanese children begin the arduous task of memorizing the essential 2,000 Chinese characters (kanji) used in the Japanese language. This task continues through junior high school, with continual drill and practice so that each stroke will be automatically sequenced and drawn.

Why is it necessary for Japanese to learn kanji when kana are sufficient for representing all words in the language? The simple answer is that kanji are necessary to reduce homonymic ambiguity. But another answer provided by Hatano is that kanji represent the "conceptual structure" of Japanese. That is, "children learn the Japanese 'formal conceptual structure' through kanji, because morphograms constitute a complex network of concepts, ideas, and beliefs — in short, a condensed set of cognitive tools of the culture" (p. 108, Chapter 5). Kanji allow direct access to this conceptual structure through their prototypal meanings. The prototypal meanings are provided by the Japanese reading of the character in contrast to the Chinese reading of the character, often called the phonetic reading. Hatano feels that this dual reading system of kanji strengthens the association between a kanji and its meaning and weakens the association between a kanji and its pronunciation. The effect on the processing of kanji is that words transcribed in kanji can readily be retrieved without mediation by phonetic codes. Hatano's research shows that kanji's "latent cognitive function" allows experts to access kanji stored in long-term memory to resolve homonymic ambiguity resulting from spoken words and words written in kana. Expertise in the Standard Japanese Orthography (SJO) also allows the use of prototypal meanings in inferring understanding of highly complex, compound kanji words.

In Chapter 6 I question the degree to which Hatano's meaning code is cognitively universal or linguistically constrained by the Japanese language. I suggest that kanji allow access to conceptual universals through their prototypal meanings provided by the Japanese reading. I point out the contribution of Hatano's chapter in explaining how kana and kanji are acquired by novices and then utilized by experts. His research on the processing of kana and kanji helps us understand the auditory demands of a syllabary and the visual demands of a logography within the context of the Japanese language and culture.

Harold Stevenson and his colleagues, Shin-ying Lee and James Stigler, explain in Chapter 7 why orthographic differences are *not* the reason for Chinese children's reading achievement being higher than American children's.

Stevenson's data are part of a cross–cultural comparison of reading and math achievement in first and fifth grade classrooms in the United States, Taiwan, and Japan (Azuma, Hakuta, & Stevenson, in press). All children were comparable on ten different cognitive tests: coding, spatial relations and perceptual speed, auditory memory, serial memory for words and numbers, verbal–spatial representation, verbal memory, vocabulary, and general information. But, on the reading and math tests, which Stevenson and his cross-national team designed, the Chinese children outperformed the American children in comprehending and reading text, as well as in math. Stevenson dismisses orthographic differences as a casual factor in the Chinese children's performance because the Japanese children in the study did not do as well on reading vocabulary as either the Chinese or American children. The Japanese children were reading the same Chinese characters as the Chinese children. In fact, the best English readers were able to read more words than the best Chinese readers, a finding that Stevenson feels supports Gleitman and Rozin's (1977) claim that alphabets are more efficient than logographs for fluent adults but make more conceptual demands on beginners. Interestingly, roughly equal percentages of American and Chinese children had real problems in reading. Three percent of Chinese fifth graders and 3.5% of American fifth graders were reading three years below grade level.

The role of orthographic differences is downplayed even further by Stevenson and his colleagues as they point to misunderstandings about the Chinese writing system. They explain that Chinese characters are logographs, not pictograms or ideographs. As logographs, the characters represent morphemes, not necessarily single words. And, of course, various combinations of morphemes will produce varied meanings and varied pronunciations. Further, Stevenson and his colleagues cite research challenging the idea that meaning is accessed directly from the visual form of the character without phonetic mediation. Such evidence seems to contradict Hatano's research on SJO experts' ability to use kanji to infer meaning directly. But kanji's inferability is achieved through the *Japanese* reading of the character although the phonetic recoding Stevenson mentions is required because some characters in the Chinese language differ only in tone.

Stevenson and his colleagues attribute the superior reading and math performance of the Chinese children to hard work and encouragement from teachers and parents. The school day and school year are longer for the Chinese student and, more time is spent on homework. American parents and teachers, on the other hand, attribute achievement to ability and do not value homework or constant attention to school tasks.

In the final chapter Alex Siegel puts Stevenson's findings in the context of the culture of schooling. He sees reading as a "many-layered thing," drawing upon "multiple knowledge bases" embedded within the culture's system of schooling. In Taiwan teachers have relatively high status and pay, parents regard school as "real business," and children demonstrate *effective* time on task. He points out that the greater variability in American reading scores raises questions about what it means to say that the Chinese children are reading better. In some senses, the variability of American scores is consistent with themes of diversity, competition (i.e., individualism), and educational placement — all valued themes in American schooling. Siegel argues that different educational systems have adaptive value in different cultures. American educators should not rush to borrow Chinese techniques for teaching reading or math, because they would be borrowing tradeoffs. And such changes might be futile, given the general level of satisfaction expressed by American parents.

The issues in learning to read raised in this volume are not new. But perhaps they have gained sharper definition by being cast in the light of cognitive universals and cultural constraints. Charles Perfetti's comments during the panel discussion at the end of the conference were particularly insightful. Perfetti reiterated his feeling that no matter what culture you are reading in, the process of lexical access, propositional encoding and text modeling go on. To this extent, what he is talking about are cognitive universals. But he feels that increasingly the action is in the cultural constraints that are provided. Certainly, different orthographies provide constraints; but Perfetti insists that until we better understand what level or what units are triggering phonological aspects, we should look for phonological processing even in nonalphabetic scripts like kanji. He goes on to say:

> I used to think that as a cognitive psychologist when I was working on something as important as reading and I asked the question of how much of the reading variability in the classroom my field could contribute and how much would be left to everybody else — motivation, classroom culture, and so on — I used to comfort myself that I was working on 5% of the variance. Now when I hear Harold Stevenson talk about the differences among Japan, Taiwan, and the United States and Giyoo Hatano talk about some interesting differences between Japan and the United States, I figure that I am down to 2% and I am happy with that.

However we juggle our percentages, the contribution of cognitive science to learning to read is profound, and the extent to which cognitive universals are "constrained" by cultural differences is the extent to which our literate minds resist embellishment.

REFERENCES

Azuma, H., Hakuta, K., & Stevenson, H. (Eds.). (In press). *Child development and education in Japan.* San Francisco: Freeman.

Bradley, L., & Bryant, P. E. (1983). Categorizing sounds and learning to read—a causal connection. *Nature, 301,* 419–421.

Bruce, D. J. (1964).The analysis of word sounds by young children. *British Journal of Educational Psychology, 34,* 158–170.

Calfee, R., Chapman, R., & Venezky, R. (1972). How a child needs to think to learn to read. In L. Gregg (Ed.), *Cognition in learning and memory.* New York: Wiley.

Frederiksen, J. R., Weaver, P. A., Waren, B. M., Gillotte, H. K., Rosebery, A. F., Freeman, B., & Goodman, L. (1983) *A componential approach to training reading skills.* (Report No. 5295). Cambridge, MA: Bolt Beranek & Newman, Inc.

Gleitman, L. R., & Rozin, P. (1977). The structure and acquisition of reading I: Relation between orthographies and the structure of language. In A. S. Reber & D. L. Scarborough (Eds.), *Toward a psychology of reading.* (pp. 1–50). Hillsdale, NJ: Lawrence Erlbaum Associates.

Kimura, Y., & Bryant, P. E. (1983). Reading and writing in English and Japanese: A cross-cultural study of young children. *British Journal of Developmental Psychology, 1,* 143–154.

Lewkowicz, N. (1980). Phonemic awareness training: What to teach and how to teach it. *Journal of Educational Psychology, 72,* 686–700.

Palincsar, A. S., & Brown, A. L. (1984). Reciprocal teaching of comprehension-fostering and monitoring activities. *Cognition and Instruction, 1,* 117–175.

Perfetti, C., Beck, I., & Hughes, C. (1981, March). *Phonemic knowledge and learning to read.* Paper presented at the meeting of the Society of Research in Child Development, Boston.

Rosner, J., & Simon, D. P. (1971). The Auditory Analysis Test: An initial report. *Journal of Learning Disabilities, 4,* 384–392.

Stanovich, K. E., Cunningham, A. E., & Cramer, B. B. (1984). Assessing phonological awareness in kindergarten children: Issues of task comparability. *Journal of Experimental Child Psychology, 38,* 175–190.

Treiman, R., & Baron, J. (1983). Phonemic-analysis training helps children benefit from spelling-sound rules. *Memory & Cognition, 11,* 382–389.

Williams, J. (1980). Teaching decoding with an emphasis on phoneme analysis and phoneme blending. *Journal of Educational Psychology, 71,* 1–15.

1 Cognitive and Linguistic Components of Reading Ability

Charles A. Perfetti
University of Pittsburgh

Whether there are cognitive universals in learning to read will doubtless prove a difficult question. However, a search for generalizations about reading processes may suggest some constraints on the form of such universals or at least may suggest what kinds of processes are candidates for universals.

There are two general questions to pose: (1) What is the nature of ability differences in reading? (2) How does a child become a skilled reader? Within each of these questions, specific possibilities concerning the role of linguistic and cognitive components will be raised. Along the way, I will draw not only on my own research, but on the advances provided in general by cognitive science. Although each conclusion will be based predominately on work with English-speaking populations, I offer all conclusions in the belief that they may, with appropriate qualification, be general.

INDIVIDUAL DIFFERENCES IN READING ABILITY

Ability differences in reading are pervasive in some nonobvious ways. We have recently begun studying two types of college-age individuals who have problems reading. One could be called a compensated adult dyslexic (CAD). He and she (we have one of each so far) have managed to hide their difficulties in reading so successfully that not only are they getting by in college, they are getting by rather well. One of the CADs is an engineer, and the other is a student in liberal arts. The first fits the high-spatial, "right-brain" syndrome fairly well—good space, good math, bad verbal. The second is more dramatic. She reads fluently under some conditions and has a large vocabulary.

We think the vocabulary, along with the heavy use of context and visual pattern recognition, is part of how she gets by. Both CADs seem to be either average or well above average in everything except reading. Eventually, we may know something about the cognitive and linguistic components of their reading ability and how they compensate for their "dyslexia." However, one thing is clear even without detailed analysis. Such individuals are scarce. I doubt that among a college population they are as frequent as one in a thousand.

Far more common is the second type individual we are studying. This is the college student low in reading skill (LRS). Unlike the uncommon CAD, LRS individuals have more pervasive problems. They are not only low in general intelligence because their reading skill lags behind their nonverbal skills, but they also are more likely than the CADs to have smaller vocabulary and to have trouble in comprehension even of spoken language. They show little evidence of compensation. Rather, they struggle with texts, as evidenced by slow reading and marginal comprehension.

One of the conclusions to come out of this work, and from much other research in reading and dyslexia, is that it is more common to find a strong association among verbal abilities than it is to find a disassociation. Verbal things, including reading, go together. The exception, such as the CAD, is interesting because it is an exception. This is the first generalization to propose: Reading ability depends to a considerable extent on general verbal abilities.

Cognitive and Linguistic Factors in LRS

What are the factors that contribute to a reading problem serious enough to be apparent but not serious enough to keep a person from going to college? The answer to this question is not completely clear. For one thing, we define the problem by reference to percentiles or other norm-referenced markers. This ensures there will be some LRS individuals by definition. For another thing, the measurements we (and cognitive studies generally) have taken have been a restricted set of tasks. In our case, we examined simple tasks of letter matching, vocalization latency, memory span, auditory same-different judgments, and a few others. These were similar to the tasks used by Jackson and McClelland (1979), Hunt (1978), and others. It is possible to discover that a certain factor is important in a skill only if experimental tasks are designed to tap it. In the case of adult reading ability, cognitive studies have been good at providing detailed analysis of reading tasks and related appropriate tasks to test possible low-level components of the task. At the same time, we have been remiss at providing analysis of *language* tasks, including spoken language comprehension, and there has been little opportunity to observe general language processing components that may affect both reading and other language processes. This is one of the needs of future research. Nevertheless, with proper caveats, there are some conclusions to draw.

The Jackson and McClelland Studies.   Jackson and McClelland (1979) used a measure of effective reading speed to reflect both comprehension accuracy and speed of reading. As defined by effective reading speed, high ability readers were in the top quartile, and low ability readers were in the bottom quartile of the population of UCSD college freshmen and sophomores. These students were given several information processing tasks designed to provide information about which basic processes were contributing to ability differences. Several conclusions from their experiments stand out: (1) ability differences were *not* associated with recognition of single letters (as measured by recognition thresholds); (2) ability differences were associated with performance on matching tasks, including the time to make a matching decision on pairs of letters (A a), pairs of synonyms, and pairs of nonlinguistic patterns; (3) ability differences were associated with listening comprehension performance, measured on texts comparable to those for the text reading task that defined the ability groups.

Results of the various tasks, including some not mentioned here, were analyzed in regression models. Jackson and McClelland concluded that there are two primary ability factors, one a general language comprehension factor that is modality-free. The other is a name retrieval factor that operates when a symbol name is retrieved from memory in response to a visual input, regardless of whether the input is linguistic. The last qualification accommodates a subsequent finding by Jackson (1980) that speed of matching, even of nonsense drawings arbitrarily associated with names, predicted ability. The cognitive processes implicated here are (1) general language comprehension ability and (2) simple symbol activation from visual input.

The Hammond Study.   A recent study by Hammond (1984) seems to modify the conclusion by Jackson and McClelland. It also demonstrates how the range of tasks used necessarily limits the range of processing generalizations that can be made. Unlike Jackson and McClelland, Hammond included a task of vocalization latency and an auditory same-different task. The vocalization latency task was used because, in our earlier studies of reading ability, it had consistently proved to be the best predictor of children's reading comprehension ability. It is simply a measure of the elapsed time between the presentation of a visual stimulus and the onset of the vocalization that produces its name. A particularly important theoretical fact in explaining children's reading ability is a finding of Perfetti, Finger, and Hogaboam (1978). They found that the reading ability of third grade subjects was predicted by their vocalization latencies to printed words but not to colors or pictures. (Vocalization latencies to digits were only weakly associated with reading skill.) Clearly, the conclusion is that linguistic inputs were critical to children's reading ability. Naming time for nonalphabetic visual stimuli was unrelated to reading ability.

This conclusion has had two points of contrast. One is with the Jackson and McClelland result previously described. Children's reading ability is associated with linguistic processes but adults' reading ability is not. Second is its contrast with the "naming deficit" observed for dyslexic children (Denckla & Rudel, 1976). This deficit includes slower than normal naming time for colors, numbers, and pictures, as well as words. This is in clear contrast to what we found in the Perfetti et al. (1978) study.

Hammond's (1984) experiment may shed some new light on these contrasts. She found that college subjects' word vocalization latencies were associated with their reading ability. She also found that digit naming latency was connected with reading ability. Thus, like young dyslexics, the college subjects of Hammond's study gave evidence of a generalized naming "deficit." This finding is compatible with the suggestion that the speed of word identification increases with age or reading experience, but within limits set by general nonlinguistic memory retrieval. The latter process is assumed to be the process by which the memory representation of any nameable (symbolic) input is retrieved. Thus, for low ability children without neurological problems, word retrieval speed has not reached the potential set by general symbol retrieval speed. For dyslexics, who may have a severe problem with symbol retrieval, and for normal adults, whose word retrieval speed has reached the potential set by symbol retrieval speed, it is the general symbol retrieval process that limits the rate of word identification. (This hypothesis is further illustrated in Perfetti [1983].) In addition, Hammond found evidence for a true decoding factor in the ability differences of this population. This was seen in latencies to pseudowords, which in a multiple regression analysis predicted reading ability independently of the other general name retrieval variables (e.g., digit naming and word reading). Thus, there may be both a general symbol retrieval factor and a true decoding factor among this population.

A second addition by Hammond (1984) to previously used tasks is also interesting. Subjects were asked to classify as "same" or "different" digitized recordings of spoken syllables, e.g., /di/ - /di/ ("same") and /di/ - /ti/ ("different"). On some trials the two syllables were spoken by the same voice. On other trials, one syllable was spoken by a female voice and one syllable was spoken by a male voice. The task was always to respond "same" or "different" on the basis of the syllable identity, not the voice. Thus, this task was a kind of acoustic analog to the visual letter match task. Hammond found that the voice made a difference, just as in the visual task letters in the same case (AA) were matched more quickly than letters in different cases (Aa). It took more time to recognize two syllables as the same when they were spoken by different voices, one male and one female, than when they were spoken by the same voice. Further, Hammond found that high ability readers were faster than low ability readers on this acoustic task. It is possible that skilled readers show some generalized linguistic abilities, beyond visual word identi-fication, that are lacking for the less skilled reader.

These data call into question the conclusion that low skill among college readers has two independent sources, one in general comprehension and the other in nonlinguistic symbol retrieval. Instead, they suggest a single modality-independent factor, associated with abstract symbol retrieval. And, because of the pseudoword differences, they also suggest a factor asso-ciated with true decoding.

Finally, a recent study by Palmer, MacLeod, and Hunt (1985) may further modify the earlier interpretation of Jackson and McClelland concerning abil-ity differences. The pattern of results Palmer and his colleagues obtained, using the kinds of tasks and regression procedures common to the McClel-land and Jackson and Hammond studies, suggest separate reading abilities in speed and comprehension. Rapid name retrieval, they conclude, is related to speed of reading but not to comprehension. The evidence again suggests that the comprehension factor is a general one, subsuming both listening compre-hension and reading comprehension.

At this point, conclusions concerning comprehension and speed factors in adult reading ability can be only tentative. Quite a bit hinges crucially on which tasks are selected and how comprehension and reading rate are meas-ured, as well as the comparability of populations. Nonetheless, there are gen-eralizations that have survived all three studies previously discussed and ad-ditional studies that are currently underway in Pittsburgh. The main con-clusion is that two general cognitive factors account for differences in reading ability among college students: Less able readers are slower to access a symbol representation in memory, and they are less able to understand spo-ken language. Both of these conclusions are in much need of further analysis. For example, it is not clear whether the symbol activation factor is general or specific to print, although, on balance, the general factor hypothesis may be more nearly correct. And we know very little about how to decompose the general comprehension factor that includes both reading and listening. Nev-ertheless, the generalizations are secure and provide part of the basis for a general theory of ability differences in adult reading.

Reading Ability or Verbal Intelligence?

One question that arises is whether the kind of ability under discussion should be considered reading ability or verbal intelligence. This question is especially important for identifying a distinct category of dyslexia in which reading disability might be an isolated problem, unconnected to other func-tioning. My earlier reference to a project on college students with reading problems was intended, in part, to emphasize the infrequency of problems unique to reading among college populations. The typical college student who does not read well is likely to have a full complement of weaknesses in verbal knowledge, including syntax, vocabulary, spelling, and composition. Accordingly, it probably does not matter too much whether we refer to differences in reading ability or to differences in verbal intelligence. It is reasonable to assume that, at this general level of skill, the verbal abilities that matter for reading are the same ones that matter for verbal intelligence.

This conclusion is consistent with a re-analysis of the Jackson and Mc-Clelland data carried out by Carroll (1980). He showed that an information processing measure of symbol memory retrieval (the letter comparison task of Posner and Mitchell [1967]) correlated almost as highly with subjects' verbal SAT scores as with their effective reading speed scores. Hunt and his colleagues have shown that performance on this letter matching task is related to measures of verbal ability, measured by SAT-like tests (Hunt, 1978). Indeed, they have emphasized the same kind of symbol retrieval process that studies of reading have implicated. Thus, at the college level reading ability and verbal ability may be approximately the same thing.

There is an important caveat to making a generalization based on these findings: There is no reason to think that they apply to noncollege adults. The reason that verbal ability and reading ability are the same thing for college students is that their academic experience allows their reading to function up to the general limits that their language ability permits. This may not hold for noncollege adults. For example, it seems not to hold for less well educated persons for whom reading lags behind spoken language comprehension (Sticht, 1979). On the other hand, it is likely that many people who show marginal literacy following normal opportunities for learning will also show marginal general verbal abilities. An interesting question, not being addressed to my knowledge, is whether such adults can continue to improve their verbal skills in the absence of reading. It is certainly possible that exposure to literate speech and demands for verbal processes (even by television) can produce a "literacy" level higher than what would be expected by low reading scores.

READING ABILITY OF CHILDREN

Differences in reading ability among children can be understood in the same terms as the adult differences. However, the cognitive and linguistic components seem diverse. If one looks with an uncritical eye at the mounds of data on children's reading ability, either a highly selective and misleading conclusion can be made, or one can conclude that ability differences in about 900 cognitive processes account for observed differences in general reading ability. One reason for beginning with an account of adult reading is that things seem simpler there. The factors identified seem generally secure, either because the number of studies is still small or because researchers entertain a narrower set of candidate component skills. In any case, it can be useful to assume that adult reading ability has, more or less, the componential character that I have described and then to ask whether children's reading ability has that same character.

Consider the child in the age range approximately 7–13, or approximately late second grade through eighth grade. Formal instruction in reading mechanics has largely ended, and ability differences are pervasive. One clear difference between these children and college adults is that the children are an unselected population. The range of ability, in absolute terms, is higher. This may be one reason it seems easier to find reading differences among children related to ability in some cognitive or linguistic task.

If we were to compare cognitive and linguistic differences between high ability and low ability readers of comparable age, we would find that low ability readers show less accurate word identification, slower word identification, less implicit knowledge of orthographic structure, less explicit knowledge of phonological structure, less working memory capacity, less use of phonetic codes in memory, smaller vocabularies, slower semantic decisions (controlling for word identification speed), less use of narrative structures, less monitoring of comprehension, less spontaneous inference making, and poorer spoken language comprehension. Of course, this list omits many other observed differences that can be derived from those listed and some that are more clearly applied to dyslexics than to the more general ability range.

One solution to this array of differences is the use of appropriate statistical procedures to reduce the vast quantity of data in individual tasks. For example, structural equation modeling provides a procedure for analyzing the contributions of multiple tasks to hypothetical causal structures. Fredericksen's (1981) research with high school readers provides a good example of this approach. Other multivariate methods — factor analysis, multiple regression, commonality analysis — can also help make sense of data. Still, these methods depend critically on choice of tasks and measurement reliability, among other things.

A complementary approach is to have a theory of the processes about which individual differences are concerned. This is the approach I take here. A model of reading ability includes the following: (1) a description of the general ability to be explained; (2) a model of the cognitive components that constitute the general ability; (3) an account of how individual differences in these components can result in general ability differences. The last component includes at least two parts: (1) a description of those components that have the potential for ability differences; (2) and assumptions about the configuration of the components in the model of ability. The following sections discuss each of these components of a model of reading ability.

THE GENERAL NATURE OF READING ABILITY

There is an issue of definition here that is more noticeable than with adult reading. One way to define reading ability is as *decoding ability,* or the skill of transforming printed words into spoken words. This decoding definition has some good arguments for it. It delineates a restricted performance and allows a restricted set of processes to be examined. However, it has limited popularity partly because it has limited application to the demands of actual reading.

The broader definition is that reading is thinking guided by print and that reading ability is skill at comprehension of texts. It is important to realize that this definition of reading, which has a long history among researchers (e.g., E. L. Thorndike, 1917; R. L. Thorndike, 1973), has both practical and theoretical problems.

The practical problem is that it places an enormous burden on the teaching of reading, and it virtually guarantees that many children will fail at reading. That is, in this broad definition, reading ability is implicated as the problem for children who fail to *learn* from reading. Children who really have trouble with reasoning or who have inadequate knowledge to understand what they are reading will be said to have a reading comprehension problem.

The theoretical problem with the thinking definition of reading is parallel to the practical problem. A theory of reading becomes necessarily a theory of inferencing, a theory of schemata, and a theory of learning. Crowder (1982), one of the few psychologists to try to stick close to a decoding definition of reading, made a relevant analogy between the "psychology of reading" and the "psychology of braille." Would the psychology of braille include such topics as inferences and script application? Such things are part of the general abilities that are applied to language use in general, and it seems superfluous to make them part of the study of braille, which perhaps should be concerned with how a reader decodes the braille into language. Crowder's point, of course, is that in principle, this is equally true of reading. The psychology of reading has become the psychology of thinking guided by print.

All of this does not matter too much so long as we agree on what we are talking about. I have generally taken the broader definition of reading ability (e.g., Perfetti, 1985), but I recognize that the narrower definition has merits.

It is correct to apply the decoding definition especially to beginning reading. There are two levels of literacy, one for each definition. Basic literacy takes the narrow definition, and intelligent literacy takes the second definition. It is particularly important to realize that, even when the broader thinking defintion is taken, the *processes* of decoding can continue to be important.

Thus, the ability to understand in children's reading, beyond the beginning stages of learning to read, is skill at comprehending text. It would not be surprising if the analysis of this ability were to uncover very general language and cognitive abilities and strategies. On the other hand, there is no reason to assume that these very general processes will be completely unrelated to decoding.

THE COMPONENTS OF GENERAL READING ABILITY

The starting point for understanding the components of reading ability is an analysis of the reading task. Of course, there are many different reading tasks, and different purposes of reading are important. However, the general case is as follows: A person reads a text — a story, a history assignment, or a newspaper — with some intention of understanding what is read and often with the intention of remembering what is read.

For purposes of simplification, the components of this task fall into three classes of *overlapping* processes. (This "overlapping" assumption is important because it reflects the continuous nature of the processing.) The reader must access words one at a time, construct temporary meaning configurations in working memory, and build and update a mental model of the text. These overlapping processes are referred to as (1) lexical access, (2) proposition encoding, and (3) text modeling, respectively. When a reader's comprehension is measured, it is usually the mental text model that must be consulted.

Each of these processes actually comprises numerous subprocesses, and there is much to say about each of them. However, my purpose here is to give a brief and simplified account of how they work within a sort of consensual cognitive model of reading.

Lexical Access

The initiating event for comprehension is the reading of words. It is difficult to overstate the importance of lexical access because it is the central recurring part of reading.

The impression that words in a text are only sparsely sampled seems to have persisted for some time in the popular mind and even among reading educators and reading researchers. It is possible to lay to rest the idea that the reader skips over words, at least if he or she is reading for comprehension. In fact, eye movement studies seem to demonstrate that the reader fixates approximately three out of every four content words and nearly half of the function words in a text (Carpenter & Just, 1981). Furthermore, this high fixation rate does not seem to be affected very much by whether a cowboy story or a scientific text is being read (Just, Carpenter, & Masson, 1982).

Of course, these sampling rates are affected by the intentions of the reader. A reader who is "skimming" makes fewer fixations than a reader who expects to be quizzed on what is read. Also, trained speed readers make fewer fixations. However, neither skimming nor reading produces patterns of fixations that are dramatically different from normal. Moreover, skimmers and speed readers are generally unable to answer questions based on text segments that they have not fixated.

The reasons for this rather dense word sampling rate lie in the limitations of the perceptual span. Readers do not obtain every much information from a text beyond the center of a fixation. Rayner's (1975) estimation that the span of perception for accurate word identification is about three or four spaces to the right of the fixation has held up rather well over several years of research on this problem (c.f., McConkie, 1982; Rayner, Well, Pollatsek, & Betera, 1982). So, too, has the estimation that information about word shape and letter identification is obtained farther into the periphery, about 12 spaces. However, such information is not sufficient for word identification. There is now evidence that a reader may be, in a sense, processing two words at a time, accessing one and having the other automatically pre-activated. A word on the periphery of the one currently fixated may have its letter preactivated parafoveally, thus reducing the fixation time when the word is fixated (Rayner et al., 1982). However, overall, the generalization is that reading is a plodding affair in which many words are fixated.

Context in Lexical Access.   Context plays a critical role in word reading, as many demonstrations have shown. However, its role in lexical access seems to be more restricted than is commonly assumed. There are two possible effects of context on word fixations. A predictable context can reduce the probability of word fixation or it can reduce the duration of a fixation. Zola (1979; reported in McConkie & Zola, 1981) found that readers did not skip words that were highly predictable because of context, but he did find a reduction in the fixation duration of about 14 msecs. On the other hand, Ehrlich & Rayner (1981) found that the probability of fixation was also reduced by context. It appears that if a word is relatively long, skipping it altogether is unlikely, and this fact may be responsible for such variation in results. However, even in the Ehrlich and Rayner study the probability of fixation remained very high (about 50%) even when it was very predictable. The conclusion has to be that the predictability of a word due to context has limited effects on access. It presumably has profound effects on the reader's encoding of propositions, because it enables an easy meaning assignment to the word being processed, but it does not eliminate the necessity of lexical access.

Proposition Encoding

Lexical access yields immediate conceptual information stored with the word in memory, as well as other information, especially phonetic or name information. This semantic encoding of the conceptual features along with the name code enables the assembly of propositions. The propositions are elementary units of relational meaning obtained from sentences a few words at a time. These units are predicate-based, linking verbal or other relational units to nouns or larger units (other propositions). (It is not clear that they should be anything like the formal propositions based on predicate calculus, and their formal status is unclear, as is the use of algorithmic procedures to define them.) However, the important point for a theory of reading ability is that predicate-like structures are constructed as a continuous part of reading. The model of Kintsch and van Dijk (1978) explains how these structures are linked together into integrated text representations.

One important fact about proposition encoding is that it takes place within the limits of working memory. The reader constructs a low level coherent text structure by linking propositions together. If the necessary linkage is available in memory, this can be done without effort and without memory search. If linking structures are not in memory, because the reader's working memory capacity is limited, because other reading processes have changed the contents of working memory, or because the text is written in such a way that information is not active in memory when it needs to be, the result is a less fluent process of establishing links on the basis of memory searches or inferences.

Text Modeling

The third component is the construction of a more global mental model of the text. This model is updated continuously in response to the propositions that are encoded. It is in the text modeling processes that the role of larger conceptual structures, schemata, become especially important. These structures include specific knowledge with which to link the text content knowledge, for example, baseball for a baseball text (Spilich, Vesonder, Chiesi, & Voss, 1979), and very generalized structures to organize event sequences described in the text, for example, scripts for mundane events (Bower, Black, & Turner, 1979). These processes may also include active hypotheses about the overall structure of the event-world being described by the text (Collins, Brown, & Larkin, 1980). The glue for the text model is the inferences the reader makes to link information in the text with his or her knowledge. It is a truism that there is not enough information in even the most explicit texts to allow full and unambiguous comprehension.

ABILITY DIFFERENCES IN THE COMPONENTS OF READING

With the preceding as a brief summary of the components of reading, the question becomes, which ones produce variations in general reading ability? The candidate processes are lexical access, working memory, and schemata (knowledge) utilization. Lexical access obviously influences all other reading processes. Working memory affects proposition encoding, and schemata utilization affects text modeling. In fact, if one looks for a unitary explanation of reading ability, each of these is a candidate.

Schemata

Schemata are critical for comprehension. There are many demonstrations of failure at comprehension that occur because a reader or listener lacks the knowledge necessary for comprehension. These demonstrations include defective texts, written to be vague and comprehensible only with additional information concerning the topic (Bransford & Johnson, 1973). However, schemata are not good candidates for reading ability differences. This is true despite the fact that individual differences in knowledge clearly exist, even dramatically so. Research by Spilich, Vesonder, Chiesi, and Voss (1979) showed that the ability to recall a passage about baseball depended on the subject's knowledge of baseball as a game structure. More important than this demonstration is the analysis of Spilich et al. showing the nature of the relevant knowledge and how it must affect comprehension. What such research demonstrates, along with related research on the importance of knowledge in text understanding (Anderson, Reynolds, Schallert, & Goetz, 1976), is that the quality of the mental text model depends on knowledge differences. For example, an individual who has knowledge of the goal structure of baseball will have it activated during baseball text processing, but this fact says nothing about reading ability. It demonstrates only specific knowlege effects. Since one individual will have knowledge structures different from another's, this does not help with a concept of general reading ability.

This point seems so obvious that it raises the question of how "schema theory" can even be applied to reading ability. The answer is that it can't, insofar as having knowledge is concerned. Naturally, the individual who has more knowledge than another will be a better reader because he or she will likely have better comprehension of most texts. But only under a trivially broad definition of reading ability is this an explanation of ability differences in reading. Clearly any contribution of schemata to reading ability will have to lie elsewhere.

The most plausible possibility is that there are individual differences in the use of schemata. Spiro (1980) has discussed several possibilities for such differences. The choice here for further explanation is interesting because it depends on a theory of what schemata are and how they work. If schemata are like possible solutions to a problem that must be retrieved from memory and examined for their appropriateness, then a search process, perhaps an effortful one, is implicated. An analogy here may be a simple algorithm for solving anagrams, in which all possible combinations of the scrambled letters are constructed and compared against a lexicon of real words. On the other hand, if schemata are like problem solving structures that are activated as part of the normal problem solution attempts, then an effortless, perhaps automatic, process is implicated. An analogy here may be an expert solving a physics problem in which the schema for the problem type is triggered by elements of the problem—because of the expert's knowledge rather than as a result of laborious search and retrieval.

No doubt there are both kinds of schematic processes—effortful search and effortless activation. But the activation mode is the most relevant for reading. In well-written texts—this is an important qualification—relevant schemata are triggered (activated) by text elements. Effortful schema search is seldom an issue except when readers encounter texts beyond their knowledge expertise. However, everyone has enough expertise for mundane texts. Thus, the reading ability hypothesis for schema theory is this: More able readers are more likely than are less able readers to have their knowledge readily triggered by texts. This is a plausible hypothesis, although one without empirical support. Support will be difficult if we keep a strict separation of the two components of knowledge—having it and using it. It requires that two readers have qualitatively comparable knowledge structures, otherwise we are not dealing with general ability but with specific knowledge. The quality of knowledge representation may turn out to be the key to reading ability in a general way but not in specific content knowledge.

One additional possibility for schema knowledge must be briefly mentioned. Schemata for stories offer a possibility for individual differences, as do schemata for other text types. Story grammars are especially relevant because children spend a lot of time reading stories in the elementary grades and because there has been much work in the analysis of story knowledge (Mandler & Johnson, 1977; Rumelhart, 1975). Two conclusions seem correct, all things considered. One is that story knowledge is a rather poor candidate for profound individual differences in general, at least when compared with other kinds of knowledge. The other is that *application* of this knowledge may be a matter of individual differences. There is some evidence that brief instruction in story structures can increase children's comprehension and production of stories (Fitzgerald & Speigel, 1983; Ryan, 1982). (Positive results of training are not always found [Dreher & Singer, 1980].) This suggests that activation of implicit story knowledge may not occur for some low ability readers. This may turn out to be a way to understand ability differences in other schemata. The question then will be, what causes appropriate knowledge to remain inactive during reading?

Proposition Encoding

Ability differences appear marked in the case of proposition encoding. High ability readers (ability defined by global comprehension measures) show an advantage over low ability readers in a number of tasks that reflect the ability either to encode propositions or to remember them. In order to illustrate the significance of this claim, I want to describe briefly one representative piece of research (described more fully in Perfetti, 1985).

Consider the simplest reading task that requires proposition encoding. The subject has only to decide whether a sentence such as *An apple is a fruit* or *A tree is a sport* is true. A simple model of this task performance is as follows: (1) encode the sentence; (2) retrieve information from semantic memory; (3) compare encoding (1) with representation (2). This is an example of the general verification models described by Carpenter and Just (1975), Chase and Chase (1972), and Trabasso, Rollins, and Shaughnessy (1971). Of course, things become more interesting when negative sentences are introduced, e.g., *An apple is not a fruit.* Our subjects, IQ-matched fourth graders comprising two levels of ability, verified both positive and negative sentences.

The results were that low ability readers required more time than high ability readers to verify even simple affirmative statements. Simple reaction time differences can be ruled out for these subjects on the basis of other experiments; we, therefore, are left with the three cognitive components required by the task as the source of the ability differences. On the basis of our experiments, it is not possible to eliminate retrieval and comparison processes involving semantic memory as sources of the difference. But the important point may be this: Retrieval and comparison processes, as well as the encoding processes, are proposition processes initiated by reading words. That is, normal proposition encoding in reading includes just this configuration of processes. Whatever the ultimate explanation, simple proposition encoding is clearly isolated as something carried out more quickly by high ability readers than low ability readers.

Low ability subjects also showed greater increments in decision times for false sentences and especially for negative sentences. Their troubles with false sentences are especially interesting, for it's not likely that their taxonomic knowledge was at fault—they were no less certain than high ability subjects that trees are not sports. The interesting possibility is that the fault lay with their somewhat greater dependence on context in encoding. True statements such as *An apple is a fruit* benefit from priming, or spread of activation, and make the predicate term more accessible. This context mechanism seems to be in good working order for low ability readers, but context-free lexical access, which must be used in the false sentences, is a problem (Perfetti & Roth, 1981; Stanovich, 1980). Thus, this experiment makes a necessary point. Aside from any processing complexity added by negation or falsification, the time to encode a simple proposition is correlated with more global measures of comprehension. The explanations and the consequences of this fact are of major interest.

To examine these explanations and consequences, another set of facts must be introduced. Low ability readers appear to have less functional working memory capacity than high ability readers. Although this fact doesn't show up in all memory tasks in all studies, it is seen in many studies of digit span (Moore, Kagan, Sahl, & Grant, 1982) and most clearly in situations involving memory for words and sentences, whether written or spoken (Daneman & Carpenter, 1980; Perfetti & Goldman, 1976). It is not necessary to think of this as an architectural memory limitation. In fact, it may be best not to think so inasmuch as some studies tend not to show memory differences and some studies (e.g., Perfetti & Goldman, 1976) find that memory differences are task dependent. Instead, such differences seem to derive from a functional memory factor, one that affects the reader's ability to hold and operate on verbal material.

The consequences of this factor are clear. A less able reader at any moment during reading can remember less of the text currently being read — fewer of the *words* just read and fewer of the *propositions* recently encoded — than can the more able reader. This deficit translates further into problems with text coherence. That is, a currently encoded proposition needs to be attached to a recently encoded proposition. For a low ability reader, the proposition needed for attachment is less likely to be in working memory. If text representation is coherent to that point, a search procedure can help make the link, but only with some cost to efficiency. In the worst case, the search for linkage is unsuccessful. In either case, this functional memory problem is sufficient to cause disruption of proposition encoding.

The cause of the functional memory factor can be either a factor intrinsic to memory or a factor associated with access of words. In the first case, there are individual differences in the number of symbol nodes that are activated in memory (where symbol nodes are words or phrases linked to concepts). In the second case, there are differences in the access of words, and low efficiency or slow access interferes with the current contents of memory. Separating these two classes of possibility is difficult and beyond what I can try to do here. However, I will try to make clear the lexical access hypothesis.

Lexical Access

Comprehension depends on lexical access in that lexical processes are the recurring cognitive event that initiates proposition encoding and schema activation. Thus, inefficient lexical access disrupts the temporary representation of text in working memory. This is the central claim of verbal efficiency theory (Perfetti & Lesgold, 1977, 1979; Perfetti, 1985). Individual differences in global reading ability can be due to differences in lexical access efficiency.

The evidence that the global reading comprehension ability of children is associated with differences in lexical access efficiency is substantial. It shows that, for age and IQ-matched children of different levels of reading ability, the low ability reader is less accurate than the high ability reader at identifying words and, when accuracy is controlled, slower at identifying words (Perfetti & Hogaboam, 1975). These ability differences increase as word length increases and word frequency decreases, and they are especially large when pseudowords are read (e.g., Hogaboam & Perfetti, 1978). Furthermore, these differences span the age range from children in beginning reading through the elementary grades, high school, and college. Unlike some of the other reading ability factors I have discussed, lexical processing differences are pervasive. I know of no research on reading ability that has failed to find lexical differences related to reading ability, given, of course, that such differences were looked for.

Although it hardly seems necessary to document further the strong relationship between lexical processes and children's reading comprehension, to add perspective to the point, I will briefly describe one (unpublished) study that we have carried out.

It is frequently claimed that there are children who can read words, but who can't comprehend what they read. It is true that lexical processes are not *sufficient* for comprehension, and logic certainly allows such cases. Nevertheless, they should be few, especially if we exclude children who have general language comprehension problems. We began a project to have teachers identify such cases for us. Teachers from grades two through eight at one school were asked whether they noticed children who had trouble in comprehension but who, as near as they could tell, were good at decoding words. An interesting fact is that most of the teachers seemed to know exactly what we were talking about. An exception was a second-grade teacher who thought the question was silly: "Of course, any child who can't comprehend also can't read words." This difference between primary grade teachers and upper elementary grade teachers reflects the different demands of reading between the early grades, where reading is actually taught, and the later grades, where reading problems surface mainly in subject matter reading. Overall, most teachers beyond the second grade believed that such problems were fairly common, and they were willing to identify such children for us.

For each child identified, we engaged in an elaborate procedure. We provided tests of (a) paragraph reading and listening comprehension, (b) vocabulary, and (c) word identification speed. For each grade represented by a "comprehension problem," we gave these tests to a group of *average* readers at that grade. Thus, one fifth grade comprehension problem reader was compared with a group of average fifth graders on reading comprehension, listening comprehension, vocabulary, and word identification speed. The high cost of this research (16 control subjects for one experimental subject) caused us to abandon our search for comprehension problems after testing nine children identified by teachers. All except one of the children turned out to have word identification problems that were indexed by speed measures. They were more than one standard deviation below the mean in identification speed for common words. They also tended to have less good vocabularies and to be below average in listening comprehension. The exception child turned out to be a good reader after all by our comprehension measures.

I certainly don't wish to claim on the basis of such a small sample that may not even be representative of the population of comprehension problems, that word identification problems will always be part of a comprehension problem. However, there is a compelling point. It is easy to suppose that a child has a comprehension problem in the absence of a lexical problem when informal observations are used. On the other hand, it is difficult to verify such a problem when reasonably rigorous procedures are followed. The conclusion is not that problems of "pure *reading* comprehension" do not exist, but that they are very uncommon.

The cause of lexical access problems is another matter. The possibilities include general linguistic processes, development of orthographic knowledge, and merely practice at reading. These considerations will be postponed for now.

Summary

To this point, I have considered three necessary constituents for a theory of the cognitive components of reading ability: (1) a general account of the ability to be understood; (2) a description of the components of the general ability; (3) some assumptions concerning the potential of these components for ability differences. I have claimed that all three components — text modeling, proposition encoding, and lexical access — can produce ability differences. However, the possibilities are more compelling for lexical processing differences and proposition encoding differences and less compelling for text modeling differences, provided we keep a clear focus on the definition of reading ability. The final constituent of a theory of ability is a configuration of the components.

THE CONFIGURATION OF ABILITY COMPONENTS

The way these ability components fit together has been at least implicit in the preceding section. Two possibilities are implied, at two general levels. At one level, the processing configuration and hence the ability configuration are linear. Lexical processes enable proposition encoding, which in turn enables text modeling. At another level, the processes may be more interactive. Thus text modeling can influence lexical processes and propositional encoding. Let's assume this fully interactive model is a bit closer to the truth than a one-directional linear model. At the same time, this interactive model is no more than an approximation of reality sufficient only for the general argument. For example, it remains an open question whether a text model — or some local context — actually influences lexical access or whether it influences the semantic integration processes that follow immediately after access. That is, lexical *access,* as opposed to lexical semantic integration, might be autonomous (Forster, 1979). The general point is that influences of knowledge, including the text model, make a fairly early contribution to immediate comprehension, but this contribution may not be to the reader's initial access of the word. Figure 1.1 shows the general schema for this interactive model.

In order to bring ability issues into focus, we have to assume that processing resources are allocated to the reading task. The lexical processes of the high ability reader are very efficient, i.e., low in resource demands. This enables proposition encoding, especially the integration of propositions, to attract most of the resources. Text modeling can be relatively high in resources, as when a reader has to make many inferences, or relatively low, as when a mundane but well written text is read.

The low ability reader may have trouble with all these reading constituents. As I argued in the foregoing, however, the centrality of lexical access in reading and the pervasiveness of lexical access differences related to reading ability make lexical processes especially strong candidates for universal status. The same is true for propositional encoding, which is, of course, the immedi-

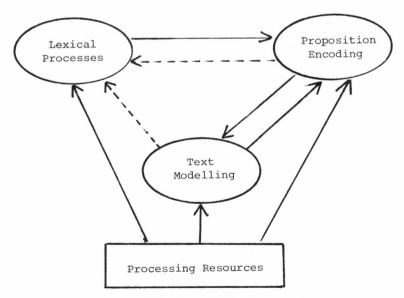

FIG. 1.1   The configuration of reading components relevant for reading ability. Processing resources can be allotted to any component. There is mutual influence between components, although the dashed lines reflect the assumption that prior direct influences on lexical access do not occur.

ate result of lexical processes. We can think of a new proposition's being encoded about every second for a skilled reader.

The final point is that the resources of low ability readers seem to be allocated heavily toward the lexical processes. Because of inefficient lexical processes, low ability readers are less able than high ability readers to apply resources to other components of text processing.

This configuration of reading ability is the one assumed by verbal efficiency theory (Perfetti, 1985; Perfetti & Lesgold, 1977, 1979). It gives a general account of the facts of reading ability by assigning central importance to facile lexical processes that operate both in word identification and in the immediate memory for words that proposition encoding entails. Thus it accounts for the two most pervasive results in reading ability research — ability differences in lexical processes and in immediate memory for spoken and written words.

On the other hand, the theory is supported largely by correlational evidence. One prediction made by the theory is that gains in the speed of word identification should lead to gains in comprehension. The predication, as far as I know, has not been given a test. Training studies that have produced only short-term gains in the word identification speed of low ability readers have failed to produce comprehension gains (e.g., Fleisher, Jenkins, & Pany, 1979). What is needed is long-term training that permanently increases word identification efficiency. This would allow the verbal efficiency prediction to be falsified. Meanwhile, there is more conclusive correlational evidence from a longitudinal study described by Lesgold and Resnick (1982). By using multiple testing points, they were able to observe measures of word reading speed and comprehension over several years. On the basis of causal path analysis, Lesgold and Resnick concluded that children's gains in word reading speed preceded (hence, enabled) gains in comprehension, rather than vice versa.

A CONTINUUM OF READING ABILITY

In this section, I turn to the question of whether the sort of reading ability under discussion is characterized by continuity or discontinuity. There are two different questions. The first is how to characterize the age-related development of reading ability within a broad range of ability. The second is how to think of reading disability with regard to a continuum of ability.

Reading Ability Through Adulthood

In an earlier section, I reviewed the state of affairs in adult reading. The conclusion was that ability differences, among college level readers at least, depended on two general factors, one simple and one undifferentiated. The simple one is the activation of a memory symbol from print, and the undifferentiated one is whatever it is that constitutes general language comprehension. However, it is possible, given recent results, that an ability beyond simple symbol activation that includes decoding may have to be added. The issue is whether there are adult abilities in decoding multi-letter strings that do not reduce to the ability to access/retrieve a single symbol (i.e., a letter).

The decoding factor is seen clearly in children, and it does not seem to reduce to a simple symbol activation, at least in general. Thus, for children, ability differences in decoding words and nonwords seem to involve knowledge of orthographic rules, accessibility of orthographic information, or knowledge of decoding rules — something beyond single letters (see Perfetti, 1983, for more on this point). Furthermore, this decoding factor is seen in high school readers of different abilities (Frederiksen, 1981). Thus, it is only among college adults that there seems to be any question regarding a decoding factor, and even here the decoding factor may be important, as Hammond's (1984) study suggests.

Insofar as the ability is speed of access to symbol information in permanent memory, a continuum of symbol access and decoding efficiency may exist. Effective word identification involves rapid access to words through printed letter sequences. This involves implicit knowledge of orthographic rules, although this knowledge of rules does not have to be represented independently of the reader's store of words. The speed with which orthographic units and related speech units (i.e., units for true decoding) can be accessed is limited by the speed of symbol access in general. The latter is the factor identified in studies of adult reading and adult verbal intelligence. For children, skill at reading is still being acquired, and the limiting effects of generalized symbol process have not been reached. Thus, true variability in decoding ability is observed. Adults, or rather *college* adults, are operating at a decoding efficiency that is limited by their general symbol access abilities. Roughly speaking, college adults are reading as well as their verbal intelligence will allow, but younger children and probably high school students are not. Thus one aspect of the continuum in ability concerns decoding and its relation to symbol access.

A second aspect of the continuum also concerns decoding but in conjunction with general language ability. As decoding ability increases, the general language comprehension factor increases in importance. One sign of this fact is the relatively small amount of verbal ability and reading ability variance accounted for by symbol retrieval (measured by the Posner task) among college adults. The shared variance between listening comprehension and reading comprehension is, by contrast, very large. There seems to be a parallel development involving decoding and language comprehension. Curtis (1980) examined components of reading ability of second-, third-, and fifth-grade children. She applied a commonality procedure to measures of word decoding speed and listening comprehension, among other measures. Two facts stand out in the present context: (1) decoding speed was very strongly associated with reading comprehension in all grades; (2) in the third grade, decoding made a statistically unique contribution to overall reading ability, but ˌby third grade, its contribution was shared with listening comprehension. Thus, somewhere in the course of reading development, perhaps between the third and fifth grade, the importance of decoding speed becomes indistinguishable from general language comprehension.

Here then is the start of a general theory of reading development. Decoding ability, the central ability in reading, develops within the limits placed by two other processes. One is a simple process of symbol activation that is not unique to the linguistic status of the symbol but may be unique to print. The second is an undifferentiated process of comprehension that is not unique to print but may be unique to language. There is much to be learned about this general language ability. It is interesting that, however it will be understood in detail, it is related to decoding. It is tempting to suggest that this relation hinges somehow on either the knowledge of the speech system or on the general nature of linguistic codes.

The Ability Continuum and Reading Disability

Is it possible that specific reading disability, or dyslexia, is part of this continuum? The typical assumption is that there is a sharp discontinuity where dyslexia is concerned. Indeed the most prevalent views of disability hypothesize qualitatively different dyslexic subtypes, clearly an assumption of discontinuity (e.g., Bakkar, 1979; Boder, 1971; Johnson & Myklebust, 1967). This issue is more complex than I can deal adequately with here (but see Perfetti, 1985); however, I want at least to suggest some reasons for thinking that the prevailing discontinuity view might not be completely correct.

The basic argument is that the vast majority of dyslexic children fit the pattern of the garden variety low ability reader. The processing dysfunctions reported over and above those of the low ability reader tend to fall into one of two categories. One is that disabled children often show a naming deficit, a generalized inability to name objects even when the input is nonlinguistic (Denckla & Rudel, 1976). This deficit shows itself in the speed of naming, just as a decoding weakness shows itself in speed of decoding. However, I have argued that decoding ability takes place within the limits of general symbol ability. The naming deficit is an example of a symbol disability. Thus this dyslexic dysfunction is part of the ability continuum. Dyslexics are along the extreme low end of general symbol abilities. Their observed decoding ability may even be close to their symbol ability, making them comparable to college adults.

The second type of dysfunction that is found more often among dyslexics than among garden-variety low ability readers is a speech-related dysfunction. At the extreme, some dyslexic children show anomolous speech identification functions, including a tendency away from the all-or-none categorical perception of stop consonants typical for normals (Godfrey, Syrdal-Lasky, Millay, & Knox, 1981). Less dramatic perhaps are syntactic dysfunctions among disabled children, including problems with the English inflection system (Fletcher et al., 1981) and less syntactically mature speech forms (Fry, Johnson, & Muehl, 1970). If the perception dysfunctions are fundamental in auditory analysis, then this certainly suggests a neurological discontinuity. Indeed, the neurological basis of acquired dyslexia seems to count against any meaningful application of a continuum to this category. However, with the caveat that neurological anomalies imply discontinuity, the speech and linguistic dysfunctions are consistent with the continuity hypothesis. This is because, for the ability continuum, general language processes set the limits for ability. Thus some dyslexics are at the extreme end of general language ability.

The continuity hypothesis seems compatible with the most prevalent classes of dysfunctions. There is one exception, however. Many disability specialists insist that there exists a subtype of dyslexia that is due to failures at holistic visual processing. For example, Boder's (1971) analysis yields a group she calls "dyseidetiks," whose trouble is seeing word gestalts. Whether such a subtype exists at all may be open to question. A number of studies have categorized subjects according to Boder's test — basically a spelling test in which the kinds of errors made, relatively phonetic vs. relatively visual, determine the subtype classification — and failed to find any evidence of processing differences between the dyseidetiks and the other subtype (the dysphonetics) (Godfrey et al., 1981; Olson, Kliegl, Davidson, & Foltz, 1985; van den Bos, 1984). Even if a qualitatively distinct visual subtype does exist, it is very small, even by Boder's analysis comprising no more than around 10% of the population of dyslexics.

Finally, the research of Gordon (1980) is relevant for this issue. Gordon examined 108 dyslexic children on a battery of tasks designed to tap analytic-sequential functioning ("left brain") on the one hand and holistic functioning ("right brain") on the other. Of the 108 dyslexics, 105 performed better on the holistic tasks than the analytic tasks. There were no left-brain dyslexics, only right-brain dyslexics.

In summary, a strong case can be made for a developmental continuum of reading ability in which decoding, the central reading ability, develops within limits set by symbol retrieval processes and general language abilities. A more tentative argument can be made to include most specific reading disabilities at the extreme low end of this continuum.

WHAT MAKES A SKILLED READER?
COGNITIVE AND LINGUISTIC COMPONENTS
OF WORD KNOWLEDGE

In this final section, I will try to correct, at least in part, certain shortcomings in the case made so far. I have argued for the centrality of lexical processes in reading ability, no matter how reading is defined, and I have suggested links between lexical processes and other cognitive and linguistic processes. The question is: What is the nature of the lexical processes that are so important for reading ability?

So far the answer to this question has been something like, lexical processes are something to do fast. This is part of the account given by verbal efficiency theory. But what is the significance of rapid word identification? One answer is that rapid word identification reflects automaticity. This is the usual interpretation. It seems to follow the spirit of LaBerge and Samuels' (1974) argument that some of the coding processes in reading can become attention free or automatic. Rapid word identification reflects the likelihood that the processes have become automatic. In fact, the resource allocation argument reflects this interpretation.

However, it is not clear that word identification is easily raised to the level of automaticity usually implied. If the criterion is that automaticity applies to a process that can carry on without affecting performance on a primary task, then word identification may not reach this level. The clear demonstrations of attention-free processing have been restricted largely to simpler processing such as letter encoding (Posner & Boies, 1971). Nevertheless, it seems that automaticity at least approximates what actually happens to word identification with sufficient practice. It may be more accurate to say that the resource demands of word identification reduce with practice, but the choice of description doesn't seem critical.

What is more important is the question of how lexical processes achieve this status. The answer must include lexical representation, not merely speed of processing. Speed of word identification is a reflection of the accessibility of a memory representation. This accessibility can be thought of in two ways: An access route or an activation link has become very effective through practice. Thus, a given string of letters activates a word representation with increasing speed because the activation links between the letter patterns and the word have become stronger with practice. This seems to be in the spirit of automaticity as it is usually understood. The second way to understand accessibility is that it represents the quality of the representation. In principle, it is difficult to distinguish between these two representations. One is described in terms of process and the other in terms of representation, but this may not be a fundamental difference. Nevertheless, I would like to argue for the representation description for two reasons. It gives a good account for accessibility, and it provides a natural link to learning.

To see the difference between the proposals, assume the word *stand* is encountered. Assume the representation system includes nodes for words, orthographic patterns, and letters. The activation link hypothesis says something like this: The letters s-t-a-n-d connect by activation links to the word *stand*. With practice, these links become more quickly activated and *stand* becomes more accessible. One thing that may happen along the way is that *st* gets activated as a pattern. However, the letters s-t-a-n-d are connected with other words besides *stand*. For example, *st*... is connected with *store, stick,* and *stone* among others. And *s* as a single word-initial letter is connected with hundreds of words. With practice the link between *st* and all words beginning with *st,* not just *stand,* will become stronger — that is, unless practice is restricted to the word *stand.* To the extent that reading includes words other than *stand,* the practice effects are general. All letter-word links are strengthened, and the reader's ability to discriminate *stone* from *stand* has not been affected. Of course, this is where links between the word and other letters come in: a-n-d will link with *stand,* but only *n* will link with *stone,,* so *stand* will be identified appropriately.

The representation perspective on this is very much the same because it assumes that letter-word links work as above. However, according to this proposal, what develops in reading are not only more active links but higher quality representation nodes, especially at the word level. It assumes that early in development, the representation of *stand* is incomplete in one or more of the following ways: (1) only the word's phonetic shape is represented; (2) only the word's graphemic spelling is represented; (3) the word's graphemic spelling or its phonetic shape (or both) is *unreliably* represented. The first two choices are presumably uncommon, although the second seems to correspond to Bryant and Bradley's (1983) observations about children who can read words that they cannot spell. The first case is simply the complete nonreader. Thus (3) in its various manifestations is the interesting case.

In the case of *stand,* it asserts something like the following: At some point in reading development, the child's representations for *stand* is as shown in Fig 1.2. It is incomplete because of its unreliable medial vowel and unreliable final consonant cluster. Concretely, this means that spelling will sometimes be successful and sometimes not. Reading, however, will often be successful, just not very efficient. The *a* in s-t-a-n-d gets linked with vowel values, a /ae/, with some unreliability because of the context-sensitive nature of grapheme-phoneme mappings. Furthermore, the unreliability of the word representation can be asymmetrical. A one-directional link can exist between the letter *a* and *stand,* allowing some activation of *stand* to occur. The argument is the same for *nd.* It is unreliably represented at the word level, but the letters can

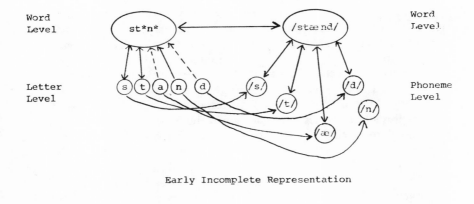

Early Incomplete Representation

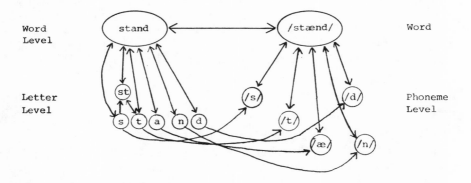

Later Complete Representation

FIG. 1.2 Hypothetical representation of lexical knowledge of a child at two levels of skill. The early representation is sufficient to "read" *stand* at least in context. But it is incomplete and, for example, will not generate accurate spelling.

activate the word to some extent, and the phoneme level can be activated as well. This seems roughly to correspond to a decoding route to lexical access.

Details aside, the main point in this proposal is that it identifies word reading ability with an increasingly refined and redundant lexical representation system. It becomes increasingly specific in terms of constituent representations — exact spellings and exact phonetic shapes replace approximate spellings and incomplete phonetic shapes. It also is highly redundant. Although the representation system can get by, in principle, without a phonetic representation, it does not, at least for a skilled reader (Perfetti & McCutchen,

1982). The redundancy of the representation system — letters, orthographic patterns, phonemes, all linked to words that have both graphemic and phonetic representation — is an important part of reading ability. It provides ample back-up representation to handle unfamiliar words.

To return to the speed of word identification, by this account, the increased specificity of lexical representation is the key to word identification speed. Word identification speed is merely the reflection of accessibility of word representations. This does not imply the disassociation of word accuracy and word speed that is sometimes implied when accuracy and speed are thought of as two different stages. The instructional objective of training speed beyond accuracy is appropriate, but it shouldn't be taken to mean that the child slow in lexical access is as likely to be as accurate as the child with faster access. Under most circumstances, accuracy problems can be found if the text is made difficult. It is the representation system that develops. Speed reflects this development.

Finally, this representation approach to the development of reading ability includes part of what is needed for a theory of learning to read. The acquisition of reading ability can be described as transitions from less complete to more complete lexical representation. To go with this description, we will need an account of the factors that promote these transitions.

UNIVERSALS?

Does anything in this account have a universal flavor, or is this merely a plausible account to apply to alphabetic systems? One candidate for a quasi-universal is verbal efficiency. The hypothesis that comprehension takes place within limits imposed by lexical processes does not seem to depend on the form of lexical representation. It applies to nonalphabetic systems as well, because it is grounded in apparently general constraints of human information processing.

A second candidate for quasi-universality is the development of lexical ability. It is constrained by general symbol activity and general language ability. All reading involves access of symbols in memory, regardless of script, so the symbol factor seems a candidate for universal status. The language ability factor has the same status. To the extent that reading is a linguistic activity, it is limited by linguistic ability. The linguistic components of reading logographic scripts such as Chinese (or Japanese kana) are sometimes underestimated. Once the symbol is activated, sequential linguistic processes dominate. Furthermore, the symbol system itself includes linguistic components. It just doesn't have graphemes and hence no grapheme-phoneme mappings.

This brings us to the final candidate, the least likely to be universal — the lexical representation system. Surely, the account of the preceding section is restricted to alphabetic orthographies. It cannot apply to Chinese, which has no graphemes, and perhaps not to Japanese, which has a mixed system of syllabary and logographic script. On the other hand, it pays to look beneath the surface. The "architecture" of the representation system may be fairly general — constituents linked to words that have both phonetic and visual (as well as semantic) representations. The particular script–language pairing fills in the details of the given system. These details are far from trivial, of course, and they have the potential to produce dramatic differences in how reading is learned.

CONCLUSION

I began by referring to adult dyslexics to indicate the great variety of reading ability. There is still much to understand about some of this variety. However, the range of reading ability that encompasses most individuals and perhaps even 95 out of every 100 readers of low ability can be explained by reference to processes of symbol activation and language ability. These processes set the limits on lexical processes that are at the heart of reading ability. This is true whether we define reading to include comprehension or restrict it to decoding. The efficiency of lexical process is important for comprehension, as verbal efficiency theory has claimed. The key theoretical construct may be lexical representation. Specific and redundant representation systems develop with reading skill. This may apply in general, though not in detail, to writing systems other than alphabetic ones.

What remain most in need of answers are these two questions: Exactly what are the language abilities that are so important? How does a learner move from incomplete to more complete representation systems? The latter question especially is of central importance to the theory and practice of reading instruction.

ACKNOWLEDGMENTS

Preparation of this manuscript and the author's research cited in it are supported in part by the Learning Research and Development Center, which is supported in part by the National Institute of Education.

REFERENCES

Anderson, R. C., Reynolds, R.E., Schallert, D. L., & Goetz, T. E. (1976). *Frameworks for comprehending discourse* (Technical Report No. 12). Urbana, IL: University of Illinois, Laboratory for Cognitive Studies in Education.

Bakker, D. J. (1970). Hemispheric differences and reading strategies: Two dyslexias? *Bulletin of the Orton Society, 29,* 84–100.

Boder, E. (1971). Developmental dyslexia: Prevailing diagnostic concepts and a new diagnostic approach. In H. R. Mykelbust (Ed.), *Progress in learning disabilities, 2.* (pp. 293–321). New York: Gurne & Stratton.

Bower, G. H., Black, J. B., & Burner, T. J. (1979). Scripts in memory for text. *Cognitive Psychology, 11,* 177–220.

Bradley, L., & Bryant, P. E. *(1983). Categorizing sounds and learning to read—a causal connection. Nature, 301,* 419–421.

Bransford, J. D., & Johnson, M. K. (1973). Considerations of some problems of comprehension. In W. G. Chase (Ed.), *Visual information processing.* (pp. 383–438). New York: Academic Press.

Bryant, P. E., & Bradley, L. (1983). Why children sometimes write words which they do not read. In U. Frith (Ed.), *Cognitive processes in spelling* (pp. 355–370). London: Academic Press.

Carpenter, P. A., & Just, M. A. (1975). Sentence comprehension: A psycholinguistic processing model of verification. *Psychology Review, 82,* 45–73.

Carpenter, P. A., & Just, M. A. (1981). Cognitive processes in reading: Models based on readers' eye fixations. In A. M. Lesgold & C. A. Perfetti (Eds.), *Interactive processes in reading* (pp. 177–213). Hillsdale, NJ: Lawrence Erlbaum Associates.

Carroll, J. B., (1980). *Individual difference relations in psychometric and experimental cognitive tasks.* Chapel Hill, NC: University of North Carolina, L. L. Thurstone Psychometric Laboratory, Rep. No. 163.

Clark, H. H., & Chase, W. G. (1972). On the process of comparing sentences against pictures. *Cognitive Psychology, 3,* 472–517.

Collins, A., Brown, J. S., & Larkin, K. M. (1980). Inference in text understanding In R. J. Spiro, B. C. Bruce, & W. F. Brewer (Eds), *Theoretical issues in reading comprehension.* (pp. 385–407) Hillsdale, NJ: Lawrence Erlebaum Associates.

Crowder, R. G. (1982). *The psychology of reading.* New York: Oxford University Press.

Curtis, M. E. (1980). Development of components of reading skill. *Journal of Educational Psychology, 72,* 656–669.

Daneman, M., & Carpenter, P. A. (1980). Individual differences in working memory and reading. *Journal of Verbal Learning and Verbal Behavior, 19,* 450–466.

Denckla, M. B., & Rudel, R. G. (1976). Rapid "automatized" naming (RAN): Dyslexia differentiated from other learning disabilities. *Neuropsychologia, 14,* 471–480.

Dreher, M. J., & Singer, H. (1980). Story grammar instruction unnecessary for intermediate grade students. *The Reading Teacher, 34,* 261–268.

Enrlich, S. F., & Rayner, K. (1981). Contexual effects on word perception and eye movements during reading. *Journal of Verbal Learning and Verbal Behavior, 20,* 641–655.

Fitzgerald, J., & Spiegel, D. L. (1983). Enhancing children's reading comprehension through instruction in narrative structure. *Journal of Reading Behavior, 14,* 1–18.

Fleisher, L. S., Jenkins, J. R., & Pany, D. (1979). Effects on poor readers' comprehension of training in rapid decoding. *Reading Research Quarterly,* 30–48.

Forster, K. I. (1979). Levels of processing and the structure of the language processor. In W. E. Cooper & E. C. T. Walker (Eds.), *Sentence processing: Psycholinguistic studies* (pp. 27–85). Hillsdale, NJ: Lawrence Erlbaum Associates.

Frederiksen, J. R. (1981). Sources of process interactions in reading. In A. M. Lesgold & C. A. Perfetti (Eds.), *Interactive processes in reading.* (pp. 361–385). Hillsdale, NJ: Lawrence Erlbaum Associates.

Fry, M. A., Johnson, C. S., & Muehl, S. (1970). Oral language production in relation to reading achievement among select second graders. In D. J. Bakker & P. Satz (Eds.), *Specific reading disability: Advances in theory and method.* (pp. 123–145). Rotterdam: Rotterdam University Press.

Godfrey, J. J., Syrdal-Lasky, A. K., Millay, K. K., & Knox, C. M. (1981). Performance of dyslexic children on speech perception tests. *Journal of Experimental Child Psychology, 32,* 401–414.

Gordon, H. W. (1980). Cognitive asymmetry in dyslexic families. *Neuropsychologia, 18,* 645–646.

Hammond, K. (184). *Auditory and visual memory access and decoding in college readers.* Paper presented at the annual meeting of American Educational Research Association, New Orleans, LA.

Hogaboam, T., & Perfetti, C. A. (1978). Reading skill and the role of verbal experience in decoding. *Journal of Educational Psychology, 70,* 717–729.

Hunt, E. (1978). Mechanics of verbal ability. *Psychology Review, 85,* 109–130.

Jackson, M. D. (1980). Further evidence for a relationship between memory access and reading ability. *Journal of Verbal Learning and Verbal Behavior, 19,* 683–694.

Jackson, M. D., & McClelland, J. J. (1972). Processing determinants of reading speed. *Journal of Experimental Psychology: General, 108,* 151–1811.

Johnson, D., & Myklebust, H. (1967). *Learning disabilities: Educational principles and practices.* New York: Grune & Stratton.

Just, M. A. Carpenter, P. A. & Masson, M. E. J. (1982). What eye fixations tell us about speed reading and skimming. Carnegie-Mellon University: Eye Lab Technical Report.

Kintsch, W., & van Dijk, T. A. (1978). Toward a model of text comprehension and production. *Psychological Review, 85,* 363–394.

LaBerge, P., & Samuels, S. J. (1974). Toward a theory of automatic information processing in reading. *Cognitive Psychology, 6,* 293–323.

Lesgold, A. M., & Resnick, L. B. (1982). How reading disabilities develop: Perspectives from a longitudinal study. In J. P. Das, R. Mulcahy, & A. E. Wall (Eds.), *Theory and research in learning disability.* (pp. 155–187). New York: Plenum.

Mandler, J. M., & Johnson, N. S. (1977). Remembrance of things passed: Story structure and recall. *Cognitive Psychology, 9,* 111–115.

McConkie, G. W. (1982). *Eye movements and perception during reading* (Technical Report No. 229). University of Illinois at Urbana-Champaign.

McConkie, G. W., & Zola, D. (1981). Language constraints and the functional stimulus in reading. In A. M. Lesgold & C. A. Perfetti (Eds.), *Interactive processes in reading* (pp. 155–175). Hillsdale, NJ: Lawrence Erlbaum Associates.

Moore, M. J. Kagan, J., Sahl, M., & Grant, S. (1982). Cognitive profiles in reading disability. *Genetic Psychology Monographs, 105,* 41–93.

Olson, R. K., Kliegl, R., Davidson, B. J., & Foltz, G. (1985). Individual and developmental differences in reading disability. In T. G. Waller (Ed.), *Reading research: Advances in theory and practice. vol. 4.* New York: Academic Press.

Palmer, J., MacLeod, C. M., & Hunt, E. (1985). Information processing correlates of reading. *Journal of Verbal Learning and Verbal Behavior, 24,* 59–88.

Perfetti, C. A. (1985). *Reading ability.* New York: Oxford University Press.

Perfetti, C. A. (1983). Individual differences in verbal processes. In R. Dillon & R. R. Schmeck (Eds.), *Individual differences in cognition.* (pp. 65–104). NY: Academic Press.

Perfetti, C. A., Finger, E., & Hogaboam, T. W. (1978). Sources of vocalization latency differences between skilled and less skilled young readers. *Journal of Educational Psychology, 70*(5), 730–739.

Perfetti, C. A., & Goldman, S. R. (1976). Discourse memory and reading comprehension skill. *Journal of Verbal Learning and Verbal Behavior, 14,* 33–42.

Perfetti, C. A., & Hogaboam, T. (1975). The relationship between single word decoding and reading comprehension skill. *Journal of Educational Psychology, 67,* 461–469.

Perfetti, C. A., & Lesgold, A. M. (1977). Discourse comprehension and sources of individual differences. In M. A. Just & P. A. Carpenter (Eds.), *Cognitive processes in comprehension* (pp. 141–183). Hillsdale, NJ: Lawrence Erlbaum Associates.

Perfetti, C. A., & Lesgold, A. M. (1979). Coding and comprehension in skilled reading and implications for reading instruction. In L. B. Resnick & P. A. Weaver (Eds.), *Theory and practice of early reading, 1,* (pp. 60–84). Hillsdale, NJ: Lawrence Erlbaum Associates.

Perfetti, C. A., & McCutcheon, D. (1982). Speech processes in reading. In N. Lass (Ed.), *Speech and language: Advances in basic research and practice, vol. 7,* (pp. 237–269). New York: Academic Press.

Perfetti, C. A., & Roth, S. F. (1981). Some of the interactive processes in reading and their role in reading skill. In A. M. Lesgold & C. A. Perfetti (Eds.), *Interactive processes in reading* (pp. 269–297). Hillsdale, NJ: Lawrence Erlbaum Associates.

Posner, M. I., & Boies, S. J. (1971). Components of attention. *Psychology Review, 78,* 391–408.

Posner, M. I., & Mitchell, R. (1967). Chronometric analysis of classification. *Psychology Review, 74,* 392–402.

Rayner, K. (1975). The perceptual span and peripheral cues in reading. *Cognitive Psychology, 7,* 65–81.

Rayner, K. Well, A. D., Pollatsek, A., & Bertera, J. H. (1982). The availability of useful information to the right of fixation in reading. *Perception and Psychophysics, 31,* 537–550.

Rumelhart, D. E. (1975). Notes on schema for stories. In D. Bobrow & A. Collins (Eds.), *Representation and understanding: Studies in cognitive science.* (pp. 211–236). New York: Academic Press.

Ryan, E. B. (1981). Identifying and remediating failures in reading comprehension: Toward an instructional approach for poor comprehenders. In G. E. MacKinnon & T. G. Waller (Eds.), *Advances in reading research, 3.* (pp. 224–262). New York: Academic Press.

Spilich, G. J. Vesonder, G. T., Chiesi, H. L., & Voss, J. F. (1979). Text-processing of domain-related information for individuals with high and low domain knowledge. *Journal of Verbal Learning and Verbal Behavior, 18,* 275–290.

Spiro, R. J. (1980). Constructive processes in prose comprehension and recall. In R. J. Spiro, B. C. Bruce, & W. F. Brewer (Eds.), *Theoretical issues in reading comprehension* (pp. 245–278). Hillsdale, NJ: Lawrence Erlbaum Associates.

Stanovich, K. E. (1980). Toward an interactive-compensatory model of individual differences in the development of reading fluency. *Reading Research Quarterly, 16,* 32–71.

Sticht, T. G. (1979). Applications of the Audread model to reading evaluation and instruction. In L. B. Resnick & P. A. Weaver (Eds.), *Theory and practice of early reading, 1* (pp. 209–224). Hillsdale, NJ: Lawrence Erlbaum Associates.

Thorndike, E. L. (1971). Reading as reasoning: A study of mistakes in paragraph reading. *Journal of Educational Psychology, 8,* 323–332.

Thorndike, R. L. (1973). Reading as reasoning. *Reading Research Quarterly, 2,* 135–147.

Trabasso, T., Rollins, H., & Shaughnessy, E. (1971). Storage and verification stages in processing concepts. *Cognitive Psychology, 2,* 239–289.

van den Bos, K. P. (1984). Letter processing in dyslexic subgroups. *Annals of dyslexia, 34,* 179–194.

Zola, D. (1979). *The perception of words in reading.* Paper presented at the meeting of the Psychonomic Society, Phoenix, Arizona.

2 Some Reflections on Verbal Efficiency Theory

Elizabeth Ghatala
University of Houston

For many years now, Perfetti and his associates at Pittsburgh have been concerned with the issue of individual differences in reading. In his paper, we have been treated to the latest conceptualization of a model of the reading process that is intended to account for those differences.

The perspective that I bring to my role of discussant of Perfetti's work is that of an educational psychologist interested primarily in children's acquisition and retention of verbal material, with the major goal of identifying conditions that optimize children's learning. In other words my interests have centered more on questions related to learning from reading or other input modes than on learning to read. I would like first to summarize briefly some research concerning learning from reading and then return to a discussion of Perfetti's model within that context.

If contemporary cognitive theory and research has identified any one principle that has been embraced by researchers interested in learning and retention, it is that, other things being equal, people learn and remember more when conditions require them to meaningfully process the material. In fact, the wealth of evidence supporting the benefits of an emphasis on meaning has led one educational psychologist, R. C. Anderson, (cf., Anderson, Mason, & Shirey, 1983) to proclaim an empirical law—the law of meaningful processing.

Typically, studies documenting the meaningful processing principle have contrasted conditions that promote meaningful processing of the material with conditions that either do not promote meaningful processing or in fact inhibit it. By way of illustration let me just sample some of this voluminous literature. Many studies have found, for example, that retention of word lists is markedly better for subjects performing semantic judgments as individual words are presented than for subjects performing graphemic or phonemic judgments. This is true for adults (e.g., Craik & Tulving, 1975) as well as children (e.g., Ghatala, Carbonari, & Bobele, 1980).

Numerous experiments have examined the effects of meaningful processing on sentence learning and retention. Again, results indicate that recall is excellent when subjects are set to meaningfully process a sentence in different ways, such as generating a missing word for a sentence (Anderson, Goldberg, & Hidde, 1971; Ghatala, 1981, 1983); generating an elaboration (Bobrow & Bower, 1969) or an image (Bull & Wittrock, 1973) for the sentence; or rating the imageability (Anderson & Hidde, 1971) or comprehensibility of sentences (Ghatala, 1981, 1983). In comparison, recall is far poorer for subjects given equivalent exposure to sentences but not required to process their meaning.

Finally, research consistently indicates that conditions that promote meaningful processing facilitate learning from connected text. Both children and adults show better learning and remembering of the information in a text when they construct imaginal representations of textual information, respond to questions that require comprehension–level processing of the text, paraphrase the text, generate logical extensions of the text, or judge inferences from the text — all activities that require meaningful processing (cf., Doctorow, Wittrock, & Marks, 1978; Glover, Brunning, & Blake, 1982; Guttman, Levin, & Pressley, 1977; Watts & Anderson, 1971).

In summary, the evidence indicates that over a wide range of verbal tasks, including word lists, sentences, and prose passages, performance is strongly facilitated by diverse procedures that have in common the requirement that subjects meaningfully process the material. Why this is so has been a matter of theoretical controversy. Craik and Lockhart (1972) originally proposed what they called "levels of processing" theory, in which the basic notion was that written language is analyzed on several levels — graphemic, phonemic and semantic — and that each level of analysis leaves a trace in memory. The "deeper" (i.e., the more semantic) the analysis, the more enduring the trace. Criticisms of this position, largely revolving around its circularity due to an inability to define "depth" independently of memory performance (cf., Baddeley, 1978), led to various revisions of this formulation that now speak of distinctiveness and semantic elaboration (e.g., Craik & Tulving, 1975; Eysenck, 1979; Jacoby & Craik, 1979). Semantic elaboration refers to the subjects' drawing connections between the presented material and existing knowledge. Research indicates that it is not so much the quantity of semantic elaboration that influences retention but rather the quality of the elaboration. That is, to be effective elaboration must clarify the concepts in the material and indicate how concepts fit together (cf., Stein & Bransford, 1979). One final fact concerning meaningful processing needs to be mentioned. Research indicates that young children and low ability persons are less likely than older or more able persons to engage spontaneously in meaningful or elaborative processing of verbal material including text material (e.g., Brown, Smiley, Day, Townsend, & Lawton, 1977; Paris & Lindauer, 1976).

Now my reason for dwelling on the role of meaningful processing in learning and retention is to point out that it is from this perspective that some psychologists (e.g., Anderson et al., 1983) urge a strong emphasis on meaning in beginning reading instruction and in ameliorating the deficiencies of older poor readers as well. From the perspective of the law of meaningful processing, although some instruction in word identification skills is seen as necessary or appropriate, instruction in comprehension processes is of major importance. Moreover, there is the suspicion, from this perspective, that consistent emphasis on word identification may divert attention from meaning and produce children who are merely "word callers" (Anderson et al., 1983).

The emphasis on meaningful processing in reading can be contrasted with the emphasis flowing from the model of reading ability presented by Perfetti. To review briefly, in the model reading is the result of processes that operate at different levels. Chief among these component processes are lexical access, propositional encoding, and text modeling. One assumption, shared with other models of the reading process (cf., Samuels & Kamil, 1984) is that reading is interactive in that different processes are responsible for providing data to and sharing data with other processes. In the verbal efficiency model, there is an asymmetry in the interaction between the components in that lexical processes are necessary for, or enable, propositional encoding, which in turn enables text modeling, but lower-level access processes do not strongly depend on these higher conceptual processes (Perfetti & Roth, 1981). Another assumption, shared with most information processing models of human performance, is that individuals possess limited amounts of processing capacity. The three components of reading are separate but interrelated tasks that require and hence compete for available processing resources. A final assumption (one shared with LaBerge & Samuels, 1974) is that decoding processes in reading can become attention free or automatic and that the extent to which decoding processes become highly efficient or automatic determines both the quality of the data supplied and the amount of processing resources that can be diverted to higher-level comprehension processes. The net effect of these assumptions is that lexical access clearly becomes the central process in reading, and comprehension results from, or at least is critically dependent upon, speedy and accurate decoding.

The model is supported by the results of extensive research by Perfetti and others into individual differences in reading ability. This research has been cogently presented by Perfetti in this volume. To summarize, the evidence shows that verbal coding facility is strongly associated with reading ability, defined in terms of comprehension test scores, for students spanning the age range from beginning readers, through elementary grades, high school, and college. Moreover, lexical processing differences appear to be invariably associated with reading ability differences. In this regard, the as yet unpublished research by Perfetti and Bell cited by Perfetti, is convincing. That is, children identified by teachers as good decoders but poor comprehenders were in fact below average in decoding when word identification speed was measured. Thus, these data suggest that, despite earlier claims to the contrary (Cromer, 1970), comprehension and decoding are not disassociated, at least when speed of decoding is considered.

Now, although the evidence for the Verbal Efficiency Model of reading ability is compelling, it is, as Perfetti acknowledges, correlational and subject to differences in interpretation. That is, it could be supposed, for example, by those persuaded by the ubiquity of the law of meaningful processing that, in fact, facility in decoding is a byproduct of reading behaviors that support high comprehension.

It seems that what is needed at this point in the evolution of Verbal Efficiency Theory is more direct evidence concerning the relationship between decoding fluency and comprehension. One source of more direct evidence comes from the type of longitudinal study wherein, by using multiple testing points and path analysis, Lesgold and Resnick (1982) were able to conclude that gains in word reading speed preceded (hence enabled) gains in comprehension rather than vice versa. Even more direct evidence might come from studies that assess the effectiveness of various types of interventions or training designed to improve the reading skills of low achieving readers. As Brown (Palincsar & Brown, 1984) has pointed out, training studies can serve as direct tests of theory involving degrees of experimental manipulation and control in an area where a great deal of data is correlational in nature. The steps involved in training research are as follows. First, the theorist speculates about the underlying processes involved in reading comprehension. In the next correlational step, students who read well are also found to perform well on the identified underlying processes, whereas poor readers experience difficulty on just these activities. Finally, students who are deficient in the underlying processes are given training to improve their use of processes theoretically specified as key activities underlying reading comprehension. Other students are not given such training. If the theory is correct (and the training is adequate), trained students' performance should become more like that of good readers.

It is clear that the types of interventions derived from Verbal Efficiency Theory will differ from those of psychologists who take the perspective that comprehension deficits stem most directly from deficiencies in subjects' ability or propensity to meaningfully process or elaborate text. The question from this latter perspective is whether students can be taught comprehension skills or strategies that will improve their comprehension ability. Numerous studies have been conducted that have attempted (with varying degrees of success) to teach students one or another comprehension strategy (see, Cook & Mayer, 1983). However, one recent training study conducted by Palincsar and Brown (1984) is well worth close examination, because not only does it provide a prototypic illustration of the type of study needed in the area of reading, but it incidentally contributes data relevant to the claims of Verbal Efficiency Theory.

Palincsar and Brown (1984) focused on teaching four skills — summarizing, questioning, clarifying, and predicting. According to their theoretical analysis (Baker & Brown, 1984), these activities, if engaged in while reading, enhance comprehension, and, at the same time, afford the student opportunity to monitor whether comprehension is occurring. Their previous research (Brown & Palincsar, 1982) had indicated that these are also the kinds of activities that poor readers do not engage in as readily as good readers. The study was thus designed to provide poor readers with explicit instruction, extensive modeling, and repeated practice in concrete versions of these activities, along with explicit instruction and feedback designed to enhance their awareness that these activities were, in fact, improving their comprehension and comprehension monitoring capabilities.

In their main study (Palincsar & Brown, 1984, study 2), seventh-grade students participated in one session per day. During the 20-day training period, students received 20–30 minutes of training on the targeted skills and then read an assessment passage different from the training passage and answered ten comprehension questions on it. The training phase was immediately followed by a maintenance phase of 5 days, during which subjects were assessed as in the baseline phase. Finally, there was a long-term follow-up that took place 8 weeks later. The major source of data was the subjects' comprehension performance on the assessment passages given on a daily basis throughout each phase of the study. Additionally, students were given transfer tasks prior to and on the termination of the study. These were tasks that demanded use of the instructed skills, such as summarizing and predicting, but were different in surface structure from the training tasks.

Now, in the context of the present discussion, characteristics of the participating students are very interesting. Initially, 41 students were identified by their teachers as being adequate decoders but poor in comprehension. One criterion for screening these nominees was an oral reading rate of at least 80 words per minute with 2 or fewer errors when reading grade appropriate material. This criterion was established in prior research (Lovitt & Hansen, 1976) as the minimum acceptable decoding fluency for instructional purposes. Sixteen of the 41 students met this criterion on an oral reading test. These students also met the criteria for poor comprehension, which included standardized reading comprehension scores at least two years below grade level. Half of these students were randomly selected to receive the training program just described, and half participated in only the baseline and maintenance assessment exercises. An additional control group of 13 average reading ability seventh graders was also included.

The results were remarkable. In contrast to the control students, who showed no improvement on the daily comprehension assessment task, all experimental students improved considerably with all but one achieving a level of between 70% to 80% correct, which was comparable to the level of the good comprehenders. Moreover, this level of performance was maintained over eight weeks. Additionally, the experimental students demonstrated an ability to transfer their acquired skills to tasks quite different from the training tasks. Finally, a posttest administration of the Gates-MacGinite indicated that four of the six experimental students showed sizeable gains on the comprehension subtest. Notably, this general pattern of positive results was found in two additional replications of the training study.

It is apparent from the Palincsar and Brown study, that interventions aimed at improving comprehension strategies and comprehension monitoring capabilities can improve performance of poor readers. This conclusion does not, of course, contradict Verbal Efficiency Theory; that theory certainly allows that improvements in any one of the interactive components in reading can lead to improved comprehension to the limit placed by the students' verbal coding efficiency. It is of interest, however, that although Palincsar and Brown's subjects possessed at least minimally adequate decoding skills by oral reading measures, they would be considered below average in decoding fluency and presumably would differ markedly from average readers on more rigorous measures of verbal coding speed used by Perfetti and Bell in assessing decoding fluency. Yet these students attained levels of comprehension performance comparable to those of average readers, but exhibited no concomitant increase in decoding fluency. That is, Palincsar and Brown report that experimental subjects' rate and accuracy on oral reading tests given throughout training remained essentially stable.

On the other hand, Palincsar and Brown identified many poor readers with such low decoding fluency that they were poor risks for comprehension-strategy training. What can be done to improve reading skills of such students? Verbal Efficiency Theory would have to predict that improving these students' decoding should allow improvements in comprehension. Training studies analogous to that of Palincsar and Brown but focused on decoding are needed to test this prediction. Perfetti's conceptualization of the type of lexical representation system that is necessary for rapid and accurate word identification should lend guidance to designing the types of instruction and practice conditions that are incorporated into such training. Given his analysis, it appears that compared to comprehension-strategy training, designers of decoding training may have some serious obstacles to overcome. One obstacle is the potentially negative effects of such training on students' motivation. That is, decoding training that is to result in automaticity of decoding will necessarily involve drill and practice, which could become tedious. Another related obstacle is that decoding training is likely to require long-term instruction — much longer than typically involved in comprehension-strategy training. According to Perfetti's analysis, fluent word processing depends on two separate levels of knowledge — knowledge of word forms, and procedures for efficient access to those word forms. The first is associated with accuracy of word identification, and the second is associated with speed. The procedures for rapid access have to apply to a well-developed lexical representation system that includes many lexical entrees, orthographic patterns, and associated phonemic patterns. This knowledge base underlying decoding is presumably built up gradually over many years and countless reading experiences, so that, in a good reader, lexical access becomes a fluent interactive process in which overlearned patterns, with redundant links involving letters and phonemes play a central role. For whatever reasons, the poor reader's reading experiences fail to build up this rich and redundant network, and it is unlikely that a few decoding lessons will remedy this situation.

A small-scale decoding training project conducted by Frederiksen and others (Frederiksen, Weaver, Waren, Gillotte, Rosebery, Freeman, & Goodman, 1983) provides some preliminary evidence that such obstacles can be overcome. Frederiksen used computer games to provide instruction on three components of reading skill — (1) perception of multi-letter units, (2) phonological decoding of orthographic information, and (3) use of context frames in accessing and integrating word meanings. On the basis of his theoretical analysis of reading, Frederiksen assumes that these three components are hierarchically ordered. The subjects were ten secondary students with very low reading skills. The objective was to increase the students' speed of processing in these three reading tasks under the assumption that this would develop the students' capacity for automatic performance. The training of each skill took place in computer games incorporating elements of competition and fantasy to maintain students' motivation over the thousands of trials that they received. Although speed was a clear objective in the games, subjects were not allowed to sacrifice accuracy for speed.

Although based on only ten subjects (only four of whom received training on all three skills), the results were encouraging but, at the same time, cautionary. The results were encouraging because all subjects who received the training game related to a particular skill, showed dramatic gains on criterion tests that required the specific skill practiced in the game. For example, subjects who were trained in phonological decoding, showed speed and accuracy gains on both a word reading task and a pseudo-word reading task, indicating that the training affected basic knowledge relevant for decoding, as well as speed. The results were cautionary because the training was specific, in that training on phonetic decoding did not transfer to performance on a task requiring a presumably lower level skill — perception of multi-letter units —

unless subjects were first trained on multi-letter perceptions. Likewise, training in the use of context in accessing word meaning did not transfer to a phonetic decoding task unless subjects were first trained on decoding. These results indicate that sequencing of instruction is critical. According to Frederiksen, direct instruction on a lower level skill such as phonetic decoding, *in a task focusing on only that skill,* is necessary before that skill can continue to improve in a higher-level task such as using context to access word meaning. However, despite the specificity of the training effects, the subjects did demonstrate impressive gains in lexical access ability. The evidence from Frederiksen's study for transfer from the word processing tasks to comprehension is less strong. This is due partly to the small number of subjects from whom comprehension gains could legitimately be expected (i.e., those completing all three training games) and partly to the less than rigorous measures of comprehension utilized in the study.

I understand that there are larger-scale training studies in progress at Pittsburgh. It is to be hoped that these studies will provide evidence for transfer to comprehension tasks that, at the very least, can refute claims that the prolonged and consistent emphasis on decoding that students receive in such training programs will produce readers who are merely "word callers." I feel sure that the evidence will be obtained.

REFERENCES

Anderson, R. C., Goldberg, S. R., & Hidde, J. L. (1971). Meaningful processing of sentences. *Journal of Educational Psychology, 62,* 395–399.

Anderson, R. C., & Hidde, J. L. (1971). Imagery and sentence learning. *Journal of Educational Psychology, 62,* 526–530.

Anderson, R. C., Mason, J., & Shirey, L. (1983). The reading group: An experimental investigation of a labyrinth (Tech. Rep. No. 271). Urbana: University of Illinois, Center for the Study of Reading.

Baddeley, A. D. (1978). The trouble with levels. *Psychological Review, 85,* 139–152.

Baker, L., & Brown, A. L. (1984). Metacognition and the reading process. In P. D. Pearson (Ed.), *A handbook of reading research* (pp. 353–94). New York: Longman.

Bobrow, S. A., & Bower, G. H. (1969). Comprehension and recall of sentences. *Journal of Experimental Psychology, 20,* 119–120.

Brown, A. L., & Palincsar, A. S. (1982). Inducing strategic learning from texts by means of informed, self-control training. *Topics in Learning and Learning Disabilities, 2*(1), 1–17.

Brown, A. L., Smiley, S. S., Day, J. D., Townsend, M. A., & Lawton, S. C. (1977). Intrusion of a thematic idea in children's comprehension and retention of stories. *Child Development, 48,* 1454–1466.

Bull, R. L., & Wittrock, M. C. (1973). Imagery in the learning of verbal definitions. *British Journal of Educational Psychology, 43,* 289–293.

Cook, L. K., & Mayer, R. E. (1983). Reading strategies training for meaningful learning from prose. In M. Pressley & J. R. Levin (Eds.), *Cognitive strategy research: Educational applications* (pp. 87–131). New York: Springer-Verlag.

Craik, F. I. M., & Lockhart, R. S. (1972). Levels of processing: A framework for memory research. *Journal of Verbal Learning and Verbal Behavior, 11,* 671–684.

Craik, F. I. M., & Tulving, E. (1975). Depth of processing and the retention of words in episodic memory. *Journal of Experimental Psychology: General, 104,* 268–294.

Cromer, W. (1970). The difference model: A new explanation for some reading difficulties. *Journal of Educational Psychology, 61,* 471–483.

Doctorow, M., Wittrock, M. C., & Marks, C. (1978). Generative processes in reading comprehension. *Journal of Educational Psychology, 70,* 109–118.

Eysenck, M. W. (1979). Depth, elaboration, and distinctiveness. In L. S. Cermak and F. I. M. Craik (Eds.), *Levels of processing in human memory.* (pp. 89–118). Hillsdale, NJ: Lawrence Erlbaum Associates.

Frederiksen, J. R., Weaver, P. A., Waren, B. M., Gillotte, H. K., Rosebery, A. F., Freeman, B., & Goodman, L. (1983). *A componential approach to training reading skills.* (Report No. 5295). Cambridge, MA: Bolt Beranek & Newman, Inc.

Ghatala, E. S. (1981). The effect of internal generation of information on memory performance. *American Journal of Psychology, 94,* 443–450.

Ghatala, E. S. (1983). When does internal generation facilitate memory for sentences? *American Journal of Psychology, 96,* 75–83.

Ghatala, E. S., Carbonari, J. P., & Bobele, L. Z. (1980). Developmental changes in incidental memory as a function of processing level, congruity and repetition. *Journal of Experimental Child Psychology, 29,* 74–87.

Glover, J. A., Brunning, R. H., & Blake, B. S. (1982). Distinctiveness of encoding and recall of text material. *Journal of Educational Psychology, 74,* 522–534.

Guttmann, J. Levin, J. R., & Pressley, M. (1977). Pictures, partial pictures, and young children's oral prose learnings. *Journal of Educational Psychology, 69,* 473–480.

Jacoby, L. L., & Craik, F. I. M. (1979). Effects of elaboration of processing at encoding and retrieval: Trace distinctiveness and recovery of initial context. In L. S. Cermak & F. I. M. Craik (Eds.), *Levels of processing in human memory.* (pp. 1–21). Hillsdale, NJ: Lawrence Erlbaum Associates.

LaBerge, D., & Samuels, S. J. (1974). Toward a theory of automatic information processing in reading. *Cognitive Psychology, 6,* 293–323.

Lesgold, A. M., & Resnick, L. (1982). How reading disabilities develop: Perspectives from a longitudinal study. In J. P. Das, R. Mulcahy, & A. E. Wall (Eds.), *Theory and research in learning disability.* (pp. 155–187). New York: Plenum.

Lovitt, T. C., & Hansen, C. L. (1976). Round one – placing the child in the right reader. *Journal of Reading Disabilities, 6,* 345–353.

Palincsar, A. S., & Brown, A. L. (1984). Reciprocal teaching of comprehension-fostering and monitoring activities. *Cognition and instruction,* 117–175.

Paris, S. G., & Lindauer, B. K. (1976). The role of inference in children's comprehension and memory for sentences. *Cognitive Psychology, 8,* 217–227.

Perfetti, C. A., & Roth, S. F. (1981). Some of the interactive processes in reading and their role in reading skill. In A. M. Lesgold & C. A. Perfetti (Eds.), *Interactive processes in reading* (pp. 269–297). Hillsdale, NJ: Lawrence Erlbaum Associates.

Samuels, S. J. & Kamil, M. L. Models of the reading process. In P. D. Pearson (Ed.) *Handbook of Reading Research* (pp. 185–224). New York: Longman.

Stein, B. S., & Bransford, J. D. (1979). Constraints on effective elaborations: Effects of precision and subject generation. *Journal of Verbal Learning and Verbal Behavior, 18,* 769–777.

Watts, G. H., & Anderson, R. C. (1971). Effects of three types of inserted questions on learning from prose. *Journal of Educational Psychology, 62,* 387–394.

3 Phonological Skills and Learning to Read and Write

Peter Bryant
University of Oxford, England

TWO WAYS OF STUDYING READING PROBLEMS

The business of learning to read and to write is not a world of its own. When children first come to grips with it, they must rely on skills they acquired long before, skills that have nothing at all to do with written words. The links go the other way as well because learning to read must have profound effects on other aspects of their lives, such as, the ways in which they think about language and, perhaps, the way they think about and marshall arguments about the world in general.

These are not controversial points. Indeed, so prevalent is agreement that reading is profoundly affected by other skills and has profound effects on them as well that no one seems to have looked at the possibility that there are some aspects of reading that are exclusive to reading and have no bearing on anything else at all. Researchers on the subject have set themselves the task, always a daunting one in psychology, of sorting out cause and effect — the determinants and the consequences of the child's progress with written language. How has this been done? How can it be done?

One of the commonest ways has been to look at reasonably intelligent children who nonetheless aren't making progress in reading or are progressing slowly. The usual argument for doing so goes like this: Poor readers are doing a great deal worse than expected and therefore must lack one of the many skills needed for learning to read or must possess it in unusually small quantities. Therefore, if we find some underlying difference between them and other children, we will know something about what determines reading.

Of course, there are other possible implications too, because research of this sort ought as well to produce practical suggestions for helping the children who fall behind.

So there is reason enough for doing research with groups of poor readers and reason too to get the experiments right. There is certainly no shortage of such experiments. Indeed the problem for anyone trying to make some sense of research on children's reading has always been the wealth, not the paucity, of evidence about differences between good and poor readers. That there is a veritable *embaras de richesse* is easy to see from any book on the subject.

Some of these books resort to listing all the empirically established differences between the two groups. Visual, auditory, cognitive, phonological differences, differences in memory, in vocabulary, in word production, in "decoding," in planning and organization. On they come like one vaudeville act after another while the spectators struggle in vain to find some semblance of a connection between them all. Other books try to make these worryingly heterogeneous and often mutually contradictory claims more coherent by whittling them down in some way, but even these attempts end up with notably broad hypotheses. Nowadays, reasonably enough, these hypotheses tend to center on language. Vellutino's (1979) idea that poor readers suffer from a deficit in language is a case in point. But I remember a philosopher, H. H. Price, writing, "When I see a tomato there is much that I can conjure." I feel the same when I hear the word "language." We need, I think, to be a bit more specific.

Perhaps the best way to begin is to start by wondering why there are so many differences — why, in other words, it has been so easy to show that children who fall behind in reading are also worse than other children on some test or other. I suggest that this is because psychologists have adopted a type of experiment that is far too kind to their hypotheses. The criticism I have to make is very simple and it even is obvious. It has been made before; but it is usually disregarded.

It is that the traditional experiment — the type that has been used most commonly in experiments that compare poor readers with good readers — confuses cause and effect. The typical design involves a comparison between two groups of children, one poor and the other normal for its age in reading. Both groups are the same age, say 10 years, and both, being normal in intelligence, also have a mental age of 10 years. They are, of course, at different levels of reading. The poor readers read no better than, say, the typical 8 year old. The other children, by definition, read at a 10 year old level.

It is this design that has produced a plethora of differences between poor readers and the rest. Let us take two examples — short term memory and the speed of word production.

It has been known for a long time that poor readers have a weak memory for words — at any rate in the short term. They remember lists of digits and lists of words, too, less effectively than normal readers do (Jorm, 1983). There is some evidence that this problem is restricted to words. Faces and other patterns that do not fall easily into verbal labels seem to cause them no particular problem. This, of course, is a brief summary of a very large number of experiments whose results are reasonably, though not entirely, consistent. It is a body of results that has led several people, most notably Jorm (1979, 1983) in Australia and Bakker (1972) in Holland, to suggest that one of the main reasons for difficulties in reading is poor memory for words.

Notice that this is a causal argument. The child who is to become the poor reader comes to the task of learning to read relatively intact from an intellectual point of view, but this child's Achilles' heal is an unusually inefficient store for words. This gets in the way when the child tries to associate written with spoken words, and, I suppose, when trying to make sense of passages of prose and necessarily remembering the beginning of each sentence as the child progresses towards the end. The hypothesis is coherent enough, but does the evidence justify it?

In my view it does not. The evidence takes the form of experiments whose design is the one I have just described. Poor readers are compared to normal readers and do consistently worse than them when asked to remember words. And, as I have said, the experimenters usually conclude that they are on to a cause of the problem.

Surely the opposite conclusion is just as plausible. We know that children do better in tests of memory as they grow older and that this improvement is particularly striking between the ages of 5 and 10 years old. It would, I think, be wrong to take this improvement entirely for granted—as though it happens automatically and inevitably. A lot of new things are happening to children during these years, and some of them might affect the way children set about remembering things. One of the most obvious new experiences is going to school, where a new and large part of the child's life will be devoted to reading and writing. Reading and writing, as we are constantly being told, do involve memory and particularly memory for words, and that means that a child who is learning to read successfully is at the same time getting practice in verbal memory. It does not seem all that implausible that the child's memory improves as a result of learning to read.

Another blatant example of exactly the same ambiguity is the much heralded demonstration that poor readers are often slower at coming up with the names of familiar things like colors or numbers (Denkla and Rudel, 1976; Ellis, 1981; Ellis and Miles, 1981; Spring and Capps, 1974). This notion has been used as evidence that these children fare badly with reading because they have a less effective language system (Vellutino, 1979). Again, the question of the causal direction is completely up in the air. It might be that poor readers are in difficulty when they read because they cannot conjure up the names of the words that they see quickly enough—this is what everyone who discusses these experiments seems to assume. But, just as likely, cause and effect could go the other way. Reading involves a great deal of practice at word production. Poor readers might be slower at producing words quickly because they have not had so much successful practice as other children have. There are no grounds for excluding this alternative or even for saying that it is any less plausible than the traditional interpretation.

Thus, in both of these cases any difference between the two groups might just as easily be consequences of the children's reading difficulty as its cause, and there is no way in which this popular type of experiment can distinguish between these two possibilities. Yet these are not isolated examples. At least 90%, and probably 99%, of the work done on children who do not read as well as they should has taken this form. The bulk of the evidence for other suggested deficits in poor readers—deficits in decoding, in verbal learning and in cognitive skills of one kind or another—comes from experiments designed in this ambiguous way. It seems unkind to say because so much work is involved, but there is nothing to be done but to ignore this work.

Yet I do not think that this experimental design should be abandoned. I simply want to make the point that, when such experiments produce positive results in the form of a difference between groups, these are uninterpretable. The design is kind—too kind—to the idea of deficits among poor readers, and ironically that is precisely why such experiments can have their uses. They are useful when they come up with negative results. When experiments that are as likely as these to produce differences between poor and good readers fail to do so, then we can be pretty sure that there is nothing to the hypothesis being pursued. There are some well-known instances of negative results of this sort—Vellutino's (1979) and others' work on visual perception, for example, and a whole series of experiments that pursued Birch's (Birch and Belmont, 1964) idea that poor readers have a particular difficulty in coordinating information from different sensory modalities. Vellutino showed convincingly that the only experiments on visual abilities which regularly produced differences between poor readers and good ones were those which involved some language as well. The purer tests of visual perception produced no consistent differences between the two groups of children. It was much the same, in the case of Birch's influential hypothesis that poor readers fail because they cannot link experiences from the two modalities, vision and hearing. The story of the fate of this hypothesis is complicated, and much of it turned on some essential controls that Birch and Belmont originally omitted (Bryant, 1975). In the end, it was demonstrated quite conclusively that poor readers have no special difficulties with tasks that involve linking visual and auditory inputs (Bryden, 1972). We can be sure that they do not suffer from a cross-modal deficit.

Does this mean that the only reason for making an experimental comparison between poor and successful readers is to dismiss such hypotheses? I think one can do much more than that, but only by turning to a different experimental design. The design that I have described can be called a mental age match (MAM). The design that I will now advocate is the reading age match (RAM), in which ten-year-old children who read no better than typical eight year olds are compared with a group of eight-year-old children who read normally for their age. Both groups then have the same reading age — in this case 8 years — and both thus are roughly at the same stage of reading.

Suppose now that in a RAM experiment you find the poor readers to be worse in some skill like memory. In this case, positive evidence can no longer be dismissed as the mere result of the poor readers' low reading level, because these poor readers read as well as the children with whom they are being compared. So positive results might very well tell us something about the reasons for the reading difficulty and thus about the determinants of reading.

On the other hand, a negative result — the poor readers' being no worse than the normal children — would be ambiguous. After all, the poor readers in this example have a reading age of 8 years but, since they are older than 8 and since their intelligence is normal, their mental age will be quite a bit higher than 8 years. This means that, in the event of a negative result in a RAM experiment, one would not be able to tell whether there really was no difference between the two groups in the skill in question or whether, on the other hand, there was a genuine difference that was concealed by the higher mental age of the poor readers.

So negative results with the MAM design and positive results with the RAM design will genuinely tell us something; *Mutatis mutandis,* positive results with MAM and negative ones with RAM experiments will tell us nothing. Comparing groups of poor and normal readers by either design is a risky and often a forlorn business.

But it is a little early for pessimism because the second type of experiment (RAM) is still a rarity. It has in fact flourished in one area only — the investigation of children's phonological skills.

Phonological Skills and the Reading Age Match

One of the things that children who are learning to read and write must do is to come to terms with the alphabet and therefore with the fact that words and syllables can be broken up into smaller units of sound, which themselves are represented by the letters. This demands some understanding of the constituent sounds in words. It is often suggested that this is a strange and unnatural demand to make of a child of five or six years, for whom the most important element in any speech is its meaning and definitely not the individual sounds within words and syllables (Gleitman and Rozin, 1977; Lundberg, 1978).

It is possible that the child's eventual awareness of the sounds in words is the product of learning to read, but there is the alternative — that children do have some of this phonological awareness before reading and that the strength of this skill plays a large role in determining how well they learn to read. Thus, it could be a cause or an effect of reading; some people think one and some the other.

The results of reading age match experiments suggest that a child's phonological awareness does affect reading — that the causal links go that way. Two experiments (Baddeley, Ellis, Miles and Lewis, 1982; Frith and Snowling, 1983) looked at children reading both real words and nonsense words like "molsmit." The rationale for using nonsense words was that they have to be read on a purely phonological basis and thus are a good test of a child's ability to use letter sound rules in reading. Both experiments compared poor readers with younger children who read at the same level and, naturally, found that both groups read real words equally well. But, in both cases, the poor readers were considerably worse with the nonsense words. Here is evidence that poor readers are at a disadvantage when they have to rely on phonological rules or analogies. This cannot be explained merely as the product of their low level of reading, because it was no lower than that of the normal readers, who managed much better.

However, the rationale that lies behind the two experiments is not exactly watertight, because children might read nonsense words by recognizing whole sequences of letters that they know from real words and work out, through a process of analogy, the sounds they make in the real word. But anyway this too would constitute a phonological code of a kind, though of a rather different kind.

Some time ago we (Bradley and Bryant, 1978) produced evidence that pointed in exactly the same direction. We got together a group of 60 ten-year-old poor readers whose reading ages were no more than seven-year-old-level — the reading age match. We gave both groups a number of tests, but the two most important, from our point of view, looked at the children's awareness of rhyme and alliteration.

In one we used the oddity principle. We read out loud four words at a time. Three of the words either rhymed (in the rhyming conditions) or started with the same sound (in the alliteration condition), while the odd one out did not. We asked the child to tell us each time which was the odd one out. The poor readers did a great deal worse in this task than the other children; they made between twice and four times as many errors as the children who read normally for their age.

In the second task, we asked the children to produce their own rhymes. They heard a single word and had to think of one that rhymed with it. Again, they were very much worse at doing this than the control group.

These are striking results, which suggest a phonological weakness among poor readers that could well be a cause of their difficulties. To see that two words start with the same sound or that they rhyme is to be aware of the sounds within words. If poor readers cannot do that well, they are probably much less aware of the sounds within words than most other children. Since they are actually worse than children of the same reading age (and a much lower mental age), their problem with sounds cannot be the product of their failure in reading. It is an illustration of the occasional power of the RAM kind of experiment.

RELATIONSHIPS BETWEEN STUDIES OF READING PROBLEMS AND NORMAL READING

Let us turn now to the wider implications of a result like this. We found out something definite about a very odd group of children, whose reading had fallen as much as three years behind. Does this tell us anything about the determinants of success and failure in the normal run of children? In other words, are we dealing with the extreme end of a continuum here or is there something idiosyncratic about our poor readers that tells us nothing about other children's reading? Before answering the question, we should define such a continuum.

It is important to realize that we are not talking about a simple variation in reading ability, going from children who read very well for their age down to those who read very badly. In the research I have discussed, the children labelled as poor readers were singled out not just because their reading was bad, but because it was much worse than it should be *given their performance in other tasks and particularly in intelligence tests.* Success in reading, as one would expect, correlates reasonably well with intelligence. So it is no surprise when a child of low intelligence falls behind in reading. The poor readers, on the other hand, are a surprise because their failures are a departure from the general relationship between how clever children are and how well they learn to read. Of course, though one might be surprised at individual cases, one should not in principle be surprised that there are discrepancies between individual children's expected reading levels (expected, that is, given their IQ) and their actual reading level. The relationship between IQ and reading is strong but not perfect, and so there must be discrepancies. Some children will do better than expected, given their age and IQ, and others worse. The degree of the discrepancies will vary. If the discrepancies are normally distributed — and a recent very impressive study of more than 8,000 children by Rodgers (1983) shows that there is a normal distribution — most of these discrepancies will be quite small, but a few children will do very much better than expected and a few (the poor readers) very much worse.

So now we can rephrase the question about the continuum. The data on the phonological difficulties of poor readers suggest an interesting hypothesis: That sensitivity to the sounds in words is one of the main reasons for discrepancies between how well children read and how well one would expect them to read given their mental age. Children who are good at isolating the sounds in words when they start school learn to read more successfully than expected, while those who are insensitive to these phonological segments do much worse than expected.

Our study of rhyme and alliteration in poor readers certainly suggests this because children who are so far behind their expected level of reading seem as weak in these skills. But, as we have remarked already, we may have encountered some idiosyncracy, some odd discontinuity, here. We cannot be sure that we have isolated a causal factor that operates right through the reading age.

There seems to be some confusion on this point. Very often people who argue that "dyslexic" children are very odd — at least as odd as those adults with brain damage who are known as "acquired dyslexics" — will at the same time also hold that the problems suffered by "developmental dyslexics" are merely an extreme form of those encountered by normal children when they learn to read. Ellis (1984), in his recent book, takes exactly this point of view. However, I cannot sympathize with this approach. Either there is a continuum, or there is not. Either these children suffer the same difficulties as all other children, but in a more extreme form, or they have quite different, idiosyncratic problems of their own. We cannot assume both possibilities are true.

For some time, the epidemiological evidence seemed to point to the second possibility — that poor readers are a distinct group and qualitatively different from the rest. The well-known Isle of Wight study (Rutter and Yule, 1975; Yule, Rutter, Berger and Thompson, 1974) suggested an odd distribution in the relationship between observed and expected (expected, that is, on the basis of the children's IQ) levels. The discrepancies between observed and expected reading levels, they reported, were not at all normal. There were considerably more children who fell very far below what would be expected of them than there were those whose reading levels were very far above expectation. This bump at the bottom does suggest a special group of poor readers who are not part of a normal continuum of discrepancy between expected and observed performance in reading. This, in turn, leads to the suspicion that their difficulties might very well be qualitatively (rather than just quantitatively) different from those of other children.

However, the test of reading used in this study was too easy, and the experimenters hit a ceiling effect that could very well account for their oddly skewed data. This objection now has some empirical force to it. A recent very large scale study by Rodgers (1983) with over 8,000 children and a reading test that did not suffer from ceiling effects produced no such bump. The discrepancies between expected and observed reading levels were distributed normally, and they gave every appearance of forming a continuum. Whatever the reasons for the problems of those at the extreme lower end — those whose reading age falls very far behind their mental age — there is no sign here that their difficulties are qualitatively different from other children's. They are probably the same, but bigger.

This suggestion is encouraging, because if it is true, the problems of poor readers are a definite clue about the factors that affect all children's reading. If there is a continuum of discrepancies between expected and observed reading levels, and if we are right in suggesting that poor readers are weak in phonological skills, then it follows that phonological skills play a major part in determining whether a child reads above, below, or at expectation. A child who has average phonological skills would read as well as his IQ suggests (other things being equal), while a child who has strong phonological skills would read at a higher level than expected, just as the child whose phonological skills are low would read worse than expected.

The data on children with reading problems certainly suggest a plausible causal hypothesis about the influence of phonological awareness on normal children when they are learning to read and to write. The next question is how to test that hypothesis directly with a wide range of normal children.

THE RIGHT TEST FOR A CAUSAL HYPOTHESIS

Our question — a very general one — is how to test a causal hypothesis about development. It is not easy to find a satisfactory answer. Causal reasoning is not a strong point among developmental psychologists. Broadly speaking, they have adopted either of two methods to pursue ideas about how one thing determines another during development. One is longitudinal and correlational, and the other involves training. Each has its strengths and each its considerable weaknesses.

The best kind of longitudinal project about a causal hypothesis on reading is a study that starts before the children begin to read. A cause must precede an effect. Therefore, you should measure the skill you think affects reading before the children go to school and then see how strongly it is related to their success in reading and writing later on. You should also, incidentally, make sure that the relation is with reading and writing in particular and not with educational progress in general. That would be a small point if it were not for the fact that until recently it was virtually ignored.

The advantage of a study of this sort is that it can establish that a relationship does exist between a skill that children master before going to school and their success in reading later on. The disadvantage is that there can be no guarantee that the relationship is a causal one. We have to worry about possibility of the *tertium quid* — the third unknown factor — which determines both factors and so causes them to be related. If you find that A predicts B, you cannot be sure that it causes B because both A and B might be influenced by a third factor, X.

A training study is a very different kettle of fish. It is an experiment, and experiments are set up to study causes. Thinking A affects reading, you give an experimental group judicious amounts of A and at the same time make sure that the control group has all the same experiences except for A itself. Then you see whether the first group learns to read more rapidly than the second. If you do find this difference, you can be sure of having established a cause. That is the great advantage of these experiments. Their great disadvantage is the risk of being artificial. What prompts a developmental change in a laboratory may have nothing at all to do with the things that really make this development happen outside. There are plenty of obvious examples in research on cognitive development. The most glaring, perhaps, concerns the well-known conservation technique developed by Piaget. There are now literally scores of successful ways of training conservation, and they make a strikingly heterogeneous group of experiments (Vuyk, 1981). Some rely on "conflict" (Inhelder, Bovet and Sinclair, 1974), some on learning set (Gelman, 1969), some on social interaction (Perret-Clermont, 1980; Russell, 1982). They all work in the experimental situation, but they cannot all be right as far as the causes of development are concerned. Some of them may indeed represent the factors that really do cause the developmental change in question. Others must be artificial, their effects confined to the experiment itself and having nothing whatsoever to do with what goes on outside the laboratory.

These criticisms of longitudinal and training studies do not, I am relieved to say, mean that one ought to abandon both methods. That would indeed be a desperate thing to do, because there is no other way to pursue causal hypotheses. To abandon these two methods then would be to give up the whole causal enterprise. Fortunately there is a solution at hand. It is to combine these two main methods. As it happens, the strengths and weaknesses of the two are complementary.

The strength of the longitudinal method is that it establishes a genuine relationship; the weakness is, as we have pointed out, that this relationship may not be causal. The pluses and minuses of the training study are the exact opposite. Its great advantage is that it does demonstrate an unambiguously causal relationship; its weakness is that this relationship may not be a genuine one. The advantages of one method make up for the weaknesses of the other. The longitudinal method establishes a genuine relationship that the training method can establish as causal. Together they provide us with a powerful and convincing way to test causal hypotheses.

A Study of Phonological Skills as a Causal Determinant of Reading

I should like to be able to describe a wealth of studies of the type I have just been advocating, but I find none, at least in the area of reading, except for the one we ourselves did recently (Bradley and Bryant, 1983). We took a fairly large group of children (403 when we started, 368 when we finished) who were four and five years old when we began our study and had not at that time begun to learn to read. The study lasted for four years, so that at the end of it the children were three to four years older than when they took our first tests. We measured their sensitivity to rhyme and to alliteration using the same oddity procedures as before. We also took a number of other measures at the same time (including EPVT, which is the British equivalent to the Peabody Picture Vocabulary Test). That was the first step in our four-year study. During those years, we combined a longitudinal study with a program of intervention.

The longitudinal part is easily described. Using standardized tests we measured the children's reading and spelling skills when they were seven years old and then again when they were eight or nine. We also gave them a standardized math test to check that the relationships were specific to reading and spelling and measured IQ using the WISC.

The results were positive. Not only did our original tests of rhyme and alliteration predict reading and spelling over the next three to four years, they did so independently of intelligence. We used fixed order multiple regressions in which the last variable to be entered was the children's performance in our original rhyme/alliteration tests and the preceding variable included their IQ and EPVT scores. It was a tough way of testing our hypothesis, but we had to do it that way to see whether the relationship existed independent of intelligence.

The relationship was independent of intelligence. Let us consider our tests of sensitivity to rhyme first. These were a consistent success. They predicted reading and spelling (with IQ and verbal ability controlled); they did not predict math. These measures of phonological awareness are definitely related to the observed/expected reading discrepancies at issue. They are related to them specifically and not to educational progress in general. The better the children did in measures of awareness of rhyme at four or five years, the more likely it was that they three to four years later would be reading better than IQ would predict. Similarly, the worse children did in the initial rhyme tasks, the more probable it was that their reading would slip behind expectation.

The initial scores in our tests of awareness of alliteration were just as strongly related to the children's progress in reading and in spelling over the next three to four years. Moreover, in one case involving the children who were four when originally tested, the relationship was again specific, that is, it was related to reading and spelling but not to math. But in another case, involving children who were five and already at school when we first saw them, the relationship was not so specific; the alliteration scores predicted these children's math just as well. When children first arrive at English schools, they are given a great deal of training in the first sounds of words (alliteration). This means that the five-year-old children who, when we tested them had been at school for a few months, must have had some of this train-ing. Our view is that with them our alliteration test was picking up not only their basic phonological skills but also their general response to education, and that is why this particular test ended up predicting math as well as reading and spelling.

This group's results with this one test was the only exception to our discov-ery of a highly specific connection between our early phonological tests and later reading and spelling skills. Overall we found a genuine and specific rela-tionship between initial sensitivity to sounds in words and success in reading years later on. But is it a causal relationship? We cannot, for the reasons given previously, be sure of the answer to this question, because we cannot exclude the *tertium quid*. Both variables in question — the child's early pho-nological skills and the child's later success in reading and spelling — could be determined by some unknown, unmeasured third factor, and not be causally connected at all.

To find out whether the connection really is a causal one we must turn to the other side of our study, the training project. From our large sample of 400 children we had selected 52 and divided them into three groups whom we trained over a two-year period when the children were six and seven years old. For simplicity's sake, I shall concentrate on only two of the groups. One was taught the skill we had measured in the first place. The children were given sets of pictures of objects whose names had sounds in common. The children were taught how to spot that common sound and say it. The other group was given exactly the same material, was seen for the same amount of time, and was taught in much the same way. But this group was taught to cat-egorize the pictures, not by sound, but conceptually, i.e., animate vs. inani-mate, and outdoor things vs. indoor things.

At the end of the project, the children in the experimental group were three to four months (the difference varied with the test used) ahead of the control group in reading and spelling. Yet the same training had no significant effect on the children's progress in math. This establishes a causal relationship, and a specific one at that, between phonological skills and reading. As we know from the longitudinal part of the study, this is not an artificial relationship. We have, I think, established a causal connection.

In some ways, the most remarkable thing about establishing that link was sorting out the methodological questions that have taken up so much of my paper so far and that have been treated so cavalierly in the past. It is difficult to find a causal hypothesis about reading in particular and one might add about children's development in general that can be taken seriously. But our results have some serious implications apart from this. We have established a skill that children have before — long before — they begin to read and that has lasting-effects on their reading. Presumably the skill is acquired, or at least fostered, by experience with word games and with nursery rhymes, even, perhaps, with commercial jingles. Presumably too it is possible to take steps to increase this kind of experience, which children give every sign of enjoying (Chukovsky, 1974). Surely this is a skill that the child builds up informally but which then has a specific effect on a specific educational task — the task of learning to read and write.

THE ROLE OF PHONOLOGICAL AND OTHER SKILLS IN CHILDREN'S READING AND SPELLING

Reading and Spelling the Same Words

The next question is how these phonological skills work. We know about the connection in principle. Now we must think about what happens when children use the skills as they actually read and spell. One thing to make clear straightaway is that they certainly use other skills as well. It would be very difficult to read English and impossible to spell it with the help of letter-sound conversion rules alone. It is far too capricious an orthography for that. At some stage, the child must also rely on knowledge of orthographic sequences and orthographic rules, on analogies about particular spelling patterns, and probably on the visual appearance of certain familiar words and letter sequences.

When we set out to look at this question (Bradley and Bryant, 1979; Bryant and Bradley, 1980), we were impressed with the transparent way in which children seemed to use a phonological code when they wrote words. Their lips would move and they would often say the individual sounds of the word before transcribing them into individual letters. It also seemed to us that nothing like this was happening when they read words and sentences. We began to wonder whether young children read and write words in different ways. So we set up the simplest of possible experiments: We gave children the same words to read on some occasions and to write on others.

We wanted to know about the relationship between words they read and words they spelled correctly. When children read and write the same word, there are four possibilities: they can both read it and spell it (RS), they can neither read nor spell it properly (R̄S̄), they can read the word but cannot spell it properly (RS̄), or they cannot read it but can spell it (R̄S). The first three categories are part of the general human experience. I know that there must be words I can neither read nor spell, and I admit that there are many words whose spelling I can never remember although I can read them perfectly well. Those kinds of discrepancies are common enough. But what about the other possible discrepancy — being able to spell some words and yet not being able to read them? That possibility seems far fetched — I don't think that there are such words as far as I am concerned. I think I can read all the words that I know how to spell.

But that turns out not to be true of six-year-old children. Many of them produced both kinds of discrepancy. They read some words but did not spell them properly, and they spelled other words without being able to read them. We found this pattern in children up to the age of seven, after which it rapidly faded out. Above that age most children could read all the words that they could spell. What does this curious two-way discrepancy in the younger children mean?

It suggests a certain independence between the two activities. If the children can read some words they cannot spell and spell others they cannot read, then they must be reading and spelling in different ways. But what are these ways? One clue is the nature of the two kinds of discrepant words — the words they tend to read but not to spell or to spell but not to read. The commonest words in the read-not-spelled category were "school, "light" and "egg," all of them highly familiar words whose spelling is not at all regular from a phonetic, letter-by-letter point of view. The commonest words in the curious spelled-not-read category were "bun," "mat" and "leg." These, in contrast, are all, from the phonetic point of view, highly regular. All this suggests that the children tended to concentrate their phonological skills on spelling and to resort to other strategies — probably to visual ones — when they read.

We did get further evidence for this idea in the same experiment: we found that prompting children to read phonologically led them to read the curious category of words they previously had not been able to read but could spell. Our maneuver here was complicated but effective. We went back to the children and gave them the words they had not been able to read before, the $\overline{R}S$ and $\overline{R}\overline{S}$ words. We embedded these words in a list of nonsense words like "wef" and "bip." We explained to the children that they had to read each word using the letter-sound correspondences. We found that this method had the effect of helping them to read the words they had spelled but not read before ($\overline{R}S$ words), but it did not improve their performance with words that previously they could neither read nor spell ($\overline{R}\overline{S}$ words). This specific effect of forcing the children to read words phonologically suggests to us that the children had, so to speak, an effective phonological code for the words they could spell. If they could spell them, they could read them phonologically, and the fact that there were some words that they could spell but not read indicated to us that children often do not read phonologically.

The Effects of Concurrent Vocalization

We obtained even more direct evidence for the idea that children spell one way and read another with the help of a technique called concurrent vocalization. This involves getting a child to repeat a word like "bla-bla" over and over again while doing some other task. The aim is to impede phonological processes. It certainly does stop the children from recognizing rhymes, as Barron and Baron (1977) showed some time ago. We (Bradley and Bryant,

1982; Bryant and Bradley, 1983) used this technique with two tasks. One was a reading task in which children were given lists of pictures with words written beside them and had to put a mark by each word that meant the same as the picture next to it. In the other task, the spelling task, the children were again given lists of pictures and had to write the name of each picture beside it.

They did both tasks under two conditions. In one they were silent, and in the other (concurrent vocalization) they repeated "bla-bla" all the time. This repeated vocalization had no effect on reading at all, but it did have a considerable effect on spelling, which they found a great deal harder and took longer to do. It appears that a technique designed to impede phonological processes impairs children's spelling more than their reading, which suggests once again that, for them, spelling is much more a phonological activity than reading is.

But there is a problem here. Spelling, and therefore writing, a word involves planning a whole set of movements, and it may have been this rather than the spelling that was interpreted by the concurrent vocalization. However, we (Kimura and Bryant, 1983) were lucky enough to find a perfect control for this in Japanese children, who have to learn to write (as well as to read) two scripts — kana, a syllabary, and kanji, which is a logographic script.

The first of these scripts involves phonological segments; the second does not, since each symbol denotes a word. If concurrent vocalization affects output in general, then it should get in the way of writing both kinds of script. If it interrupts phonological processes specifically, as we have suggested, then it will slow down writing kana but not kanji. The second result is the one that we found. We can conclude, therefore, that spelling English is interrupted by concurrent vocalization because spelling depends so much on phonological processes. In contrast, reading is not so vulnerable because it is, at first, less a phonological business.

Let me repeat that all that I have said about the apparent split between reading and spelling applies at the most to the two years or so of learning to read and to write. After that, it is plain that the two functions come much closer together and are done in much the same way. Phonological processes play a larger part than hitherto in reading, and particularly in reading unfamiliar words.

Different Phonological Tasks and Different Levels of Awareness

I should like to add a few further speculations about the causal links between phonological skills and reading. One is about the persistent claim I mentioned much earlier that phonological skills are the product of learning to read. I have produced enough evidence to show that, in their extreme form, these theories must be wrong. Some phonological awareness precedes and influences the course of reading. However, it may be wrong to talk of phonological skills as just one set of skills—there may be many. Certainly there are easy tests and harder ones. Our tests of the detection of rhyme and alliteration, which do not cause much difficulty to children who as yet know nothing of reading, can be counted as easy. But difficult tests are not hard to find. The elision task (what would the word PENNY sound like without the P sound?) invented by Bruce (1964) and developed by Rosner and Simon (1971) is one difficult test. Bruce found that children could not manage the task until several years after they had begun to learn to read. Another difficult test is the well-known Liberman, Shankweiler, Liberman, Fowler and Fischer (1978) tapping task, in which children have to tap out the number of phonemes in each of a series of words read to them. Children who have not begun to read, and many who have begun, cannot cope with this task.

Those two difficult tasks involve the child's taking into account all the sounds of the word in question. Our rhyming and alliteration tasks, on the other hand, involve a response to the sounds of only part of the word—either at its beginning or at its end. It seems possible to me that operating on one sound in one position is something that precedes reading, while working out all the sounds in a word is something the child has to learn to do while learning how to read.

CATEGORIES AND ANALOGIES

The position of the sound obviously plays an important role in tasks like ours, where words have to be put into categories on the basis of the same sounds. We already know that it is far harder for children to comprehend that "tip" and "pen" have a sound in common than that "pit" and "pen" do.

I have an idea about the detection of rhyme and alliteration. These involve two functions: one is isolating a sound in two or more words, and the other is putting words into categories on the basis of their sharing particular sounds in the same position. My idea is that the second of these is crucially important at first. Long before children begin to read or spell, they categorize words as starting or ending in the same way or even perhaps as having the same middle sound in common. When they read, they take naturally to putting words that start or end in the same way, and that therefore have the same spelling patterns, into the same categories.

This means that very young children should be able to manage some sophisticated things. One of these would be to make analogies. If children understand that words with similar sounds often have similar spelling patterns and vice versa, they should be able to use the knowledge of one written word to work out the meaning of another, completely new word that has the same spelling pattern. Not surprisingly, it has been suggested that young children are unable to make this type of analogy either when they read or when they write words (Marsh, Friedman, Welch and Desberg, 1980 and 1981).

However, we have some evidence that they are not so unskilled. Usha Goswami, who works in our department, recently showed that even six-year-old children make immediate analogies from spelling patterns they have come across with one word only. Having learned either to read or to spell the word "leak" for example, they will immediately transfer this knowledge to reading and spelling the words "beak" and "peak" and even, wrongly, to spelling "seek" and "meek." Surely this shows that they easily come to the idea that words having sounds in common also may have spelling patterns in common too. This work of Goswami's is important, partly because it flies in the face of previous claims that children make no analogies about spelling patterns until they are much older than the children whom she tested and partly because it offers us a bridge between phonological codes and complex orthographic sequences. The analogies she has discovered in such young children are quite plainly phonologically based, but they transcend single letter-sound correspondences. A child who, by knowing how to read "night," can go on to work out what "fight" means knows how to connect a sound with the whole sequence of letters "-ight."

We can conclude that the phonological skills that children develop before they begin to read, and which then affect their reading and spelling, are not just a matter of dismembering individual words into phonemes and thus learning about grapheme-phoneme correspondences. They also involve categorizing words with sounds in common and hence whose orthographic sequences are not just individual alphabetic letters.

CONCLUSION

Much of what I have said is about how to approach the problem of what determines successes and failures in learning to read and to write. If I have a central point, it is that not enough attention has been paid to obtaining good evidence on this question. The hypotheses are not the stumbling block: the problem is the research that is said to support them. The perils of experiments on backward readers that make comparisons with children of the same mental age are still widely ignored. Whole hypotheses rest, quite insecurely, on positive results from experiments using the mental age match. I have mentioned hypotheses about memory, but there are others — longitudinal studies with no element of intervention and intervention studies with no trace of a longitudinal component — that still continue to be done.

Nevertheless, the intention behind much of this sort of work was to support an idea that we ourselves have shown to be largely true. This is that a child's sensitivity to phonological processes plays an important role in learning to read and also to spell (Gleitman and Rozin, 1977; Hakes, 1980). There can be little doubt now that this is correct. But we have also demonstrated that the nature of the connection between a child's phonological sensitivity and the way that he or she copes with written language is a subtle one. The connection involves not only single letter-sound correspondences, but syllables and complex orthographic sequences as well. It calls into play impressive cognitive skills, such as analogical reasoning. It is at first much more important in children's spelling than in their reading.

None of these additional bits of information is of the slightest importance unless we can be sure that phonological awareness does play a causal role in learning to read. It is now clear that it does do that. It is in fact one determinant, and without doubt there are others too. The next step should be to use the methods we have described to identify the other causes as well.

REFERENCES

Baddeley, A., D., Ellis, N. C., Miles, T. R., & Lewis, V. J. (1982). Developmental and acquired dyslexia: A comparison. *Cognition, 11,* 185–199.

Bakker, D. J. (1972). *Temporal order in disturbed reading.* Rotterdam: Rotterdam University Press.

Barron, R., & Baron, J. (1977). How children get meaning from printed words. *Child Development, 48,* 587–594.

Birch, H., & Belmont, L. (1964). Auditory-visual integration in normal and retarded readers. *American Journal of Orthopsychiatry, 34,* 852–861.

Bradley, L., & Bryant, P. E. (1978). Difficulties in auditory organization as a possible cause of reading backwardness. *Nature, 271,* 746–747.

Bradley, L, & Bryant, P. E. (1979). The independence of reading and spelling in backward and normal readers. *Developmental Medicine and Child Neurology, 21,* 504–514.

Bradley, L., & Bryant, P. E. (1982). Reading and spelling difficulties. In J. P. Das, R. F. Mulcahy & A. E. Wall (Eds.), *Theory and research in learning disabilities.* (pp. 189–200). New York: Plenum Press.

Bradley, L., & Bryant, P. E. (1983). Categorizing sounds and learning to read—a causal connection. *Nature, 301,* 419–421.

Bruce, D. J. (1964). The analysis of word sounds by young children. *British Journal of Educational Psychology, 34,* 158–170.

Bryant, P. E. (1975). Cross-modal development and reading. In D. D. Duane & M. B. Rawson (Eds.), *Reading, perception and language.* (pp. 195–213). Baltimore: York Press.

Bryant, P. E., & Bradley, L. (1980). Why children sometimes write words which they cannot read. In U. Frith (Ed.), *Cognitive processes in spelling.* (pp. 355–372). London: Academic Press.

Bryant, P. E. & Bradley, L. (1983). Psychological strategies and the development of reading and writing. In M. Martlew (Ed.), *The psychology of written language.* (pp. 163–178). Chichester: J. Wiley.

Bryden, M. P. (1972). Auditory-visual and sequential-spatial matching in relation to reading ability. *Child Development, 43,* 824–832.

Chukovsky, K. (1974). *From two to five.* Berkeley: University of California Press.

Denckla, M. B., & Rudel, R. (1976). Rapid "automatised" naming (RAN): Dyslexia differentiated from other learning disabilities. *Neuropsychologia, 14,* 471–479.

Ellis, A. W. (1984). *Reading, writing and dyslexia.* London: Lawrence Erlbaum & Associates.

Ellis, N. (1981). Visual and name coding in dyslexic children. *Psychological Research, 43,* 201–218.

Ellis, N., & Miles, T. R. (1981). A lexical encoding deficiency I: Experimental evidence. In G. T. Pavlides & T. R. Miles (Eds.), *Dyslexia research and its applications to education.* (pp. 177–215). London: John Wiley.

Frith, U., & Snowling, M. (1983). Reading for meaning and reading for sound in autistic and dyslexic children. *British Journal of Developmental Psychology, 1,* 329–342.

Gelman, R. (1969). Conservation acquisition: A problem of learning to attend to relevant attributes. *Journal of Experimental Child Psychology, 7,* 167–187.

Gleitman, L. R., & Rozin, P. (1977). The structure and acquisition of reading I: Relations between orthographies and the structure of language. In A. S. Reber & D. L. Scarborough (Eds.), *Toward a Psychology of Reading.* (pp. 1–50). New York: Lawrence Erlbaum Associates.

Hakes, D. T. (1980). *The development of metalinguistic abilities in children.* Berlin: Springer Verlag.

Inhelder, B., Bovet, M., & Sinclair, H. (1974). *Learning and the development of cognition.* London: Routledge and Kegan Paul.

Jorm, A. F. (1979). The cognitive and neurological basis of developmental dyslexia: A theoretical framework. *Cognition, 7,* 19–33.

Jorm, A. F. (1983). Specific reading retardation and working memory: A review. *British Journal of Psychology, 74,* 311–342.

Kimura, Y., & Bryant, P. E. (1983). Reading and writing in English and Japanese. *British Journal of Developmental Psychology, 1,* 143–154.

Liberman, I. Y., Shankweiler, D., Liberman, A. M., Fowler, C., & Fischer, F. W. (1977). Phonetic segmentation and recoding in the beginning reader. In A. S. Reber & D. L. Scarborough (Eds.), *Toward a psychology of reading.* (pp. 207–227). New York: Lawrence Erlbaum Associates.

Lundberg, I. (1978). Aspects of linguistic awareness related to reading. In A. Sinclair, R. J. Jarvella & W. J. M. Levelt (Eds.), *The child's conception of language.* (pp. 83–96). Berlin: Springer Verlag.

Marsh, G., Friedman, M. P., Welch, V., & Desberg, P. (1980). Developmental strategies in spelling. In U. Frith (Ed.), *Cognitive processes in spelling.* (pp. 339–354). London: Academic Press.

Marsh, G., Friedman, M. P., Welch, V., & Desberg, P. (1981). A cognitive-developmental approach to reading acquisition. In G. E. MacKinnon & T. G. Waller (Eds.), *Reading Research. Advances in Theory and Practice, Vol. 3.* New York: Academic Press.

Perret-Clermont, A. N. (1980). *Social interaction and cognitive development in children.* London: Academic Press.

Rodgers, B. (1983). The identification and prevalence of specific reading retardation. *British Journal of Educational Psychology, 53,* 369–373.

Rosner, J. & Simon, D. P. (1971). The Auditory Analysis Test: An initial report. *Journal of Learning Disabilities, 4,* 384–392.

Russell, J. (1982). Cognitive conflict, transmission and justification: Conservation through dyadic interaction. *Journal of Genetic Psychology, 140,* 283–297.

Rutter, M., & Yule, W. (1975). The concept of specific reading retardation. *Journal of Child Psychology and Psychiatry, 16,* 181–197.

Spring, C. & Capps, C. (1974). Encoding speed, rehearsal and probed recall of dyslexic boys. *Journal of Educational Psychology, 66,* 780–786.

Vellutino, F. (1979). *Dyslexia: theory and research.* Cambridge, MA: MIT Press.

Vuyk, R. (1981). *Overview and critique of Piaget's Genetic Epistmeology 1965–1980,* Vol.2. London: Academic Press.

Yule, W., Rutter, M., Berger, M., & Thompson J. (1974). Over- and under-achievement in reading: Distribution in the general population. *British Journal of Educational Psychology, 44,* 1–12.

4 Phonological Skills and Learning to Read and Write: Reactions and Implications

Jerome Rosner
University of Houston

Professor Bryant says much that is worthy of discussion. I will limit my remarks to his explication of the relationship between phonological awareness and reading achievement. I will cite data that add strong support to the notion of a cause and effect linkup between the two — data, by the way, that appear to have been unfamiliar to Professor Bryant when he prepared his remarks. Then I will go on to propose certain practical implications; specifically, how knowledge of a child's phonological skills can help the teacher select an optimally effective reading instruction program.

To begin, a few more comments about the term phonological awareness and what it means in behavioral terms. As Bryant points out, from very early in life, the normal child learns to identify an increasing number of visual and acoustical patterns as meaningful units. In time, the child also begins to observe that these meaningful units are made up of sensory components — structural units that typically display certain features. In the visual domain, for example, the child commences to perceive people/objects as comprising a finite number of constituent parts displaying such attributes as color, size, shape, orientation, and so on. In the acoustical domain — and the only acoustical stimuli that are pertinent in this volume are those that emerge as spoken language — the child starts to recognize that spoken words consist of prescribed sequences of specific sounds that display such attributes as clarity, volume, pitch, and so on. These basic analysis abilities have been referred to as visual and auditory perceptual (or analysis) skills (Rosner, 1972).

During the late 1960s, I directed a research effort that focused on visual and auditory perceptual skills; in particular, their connection with school achievement and their modifiability (Rosner, 1969). Then, as now, much more was known about visual than about auditory skills. Many valid tests were available to assess the former, the most satisfactory for our purposes being those that compared a child's abiltiy to copy certain geometric designs with the abilities of other normal children of the same age; in operational terms, tests that evaluated the child's ability to identify and reproduce a finite number of lines of absolute and relative lengths and orientations (Koppitz, 1975; Slosson, 1967; Starr, 1961; Watkins, 1976).

Analogous tests of auditory analysis skills were unavailable. Tests that used nonverbal sounds (e.g., handclapping patterns) (Rosner, Richman & Scott, 1969) proved to be of no value. Although they often showed a positive correlation with reading, we were never able to demonstrate a transfer effect. In other words, improved ability to analyze nonverbal acoustical stimuli did not affect reading performance. In retrospect, this is not surprising. But more about that in a moment.

Spoken word discrimination tests were also insufficient to our needs. It is one thing for a child to be able to identify same and different words; it is another, and more complex task, to isolate those similarities and differences in precise ways.

Ultimately, we stumbled on the notion of sound deletion (Bruce, 1964), and conducted a series of studies that probed the linkup between a child's classroom reading achievement and the ability to analyze spoken words into phonemic units (Rosner & Simon, 1971). Stated briefly, we administered a sound deletion test to about 300 elementary school children in a suburban Pittsburgh, Pennsylvania, public school. The test contained 40 items of varying difficulty. (In fact, we did not know their relative difficulties at that time; that was one of the goals of the study.) At what turned out to be the simple level, the child was asked to repeat a two-syllable compound word (e.g., "*birthday*"), then to say it again, but without ("don't say" or "leave off") one of the syllables. Other items called for the deletion of a single syllable in a polysyllabic, noncompound word, and still others involved the deletion of a single consonant sound "Say *make*......now say it again, but don't say /m/"; "Say *please*......now say it again, but don't say /z/"; "Say *spark*......now say it again, but don't say /p/."

Test outcomes revealed that sound deletion tasks were most difficult for first-grade children, less difficult for second and third graders and not at all demanding for most children beyond fourth grade.

These same children were also given a standardized achievement test (Stanford Achievement Test, 1964) and a group IQ test (Otis-Lennon, 1964). From these data, we calculated partial correlations between reading achievement and auditory analysis skills, controlling on IQ. The partial Rs were very impressive, ranging at different grade levels from .40 to .70. We then repeated this study in other schools and obtained similar results. Clearly, there was a very strong connection between reading achievement and auditory analysis skills (as measured by the method described above) that was independent of IQ. This, however, did not permit us to infer cause and effect. More investigation was needed.

Our next step, then, was to conduct a training study to assess the effects of instruction in phonemic analysis on auditory analysis skills and on reading achievement. (Attention: Professor Bryant!) I will not attempt to describe the details of the study here (See Rosner, 1971). Rather, I will simply report the main outcomes, which were: (1) Auditory analysis skills can be taught to children who have not yet learned to read; indeed, we subsequently showed that four-year-olds profit from appropriately designed auditory analysis skills training (Rosner, 1974). Here, again, are data that disagree with Professor Bryant; this time when he argues that the sound deletion task designed by Rosner and Simon (1971) cannot be mastered by prereaders. His statement that the task requires the child to take into account all the sounds of the word in question is simply incorrect (see Rosner, 1974). (2) A child's pre-reading auditory analysis skills influence significantly subsequent achievement in reading, especially in that aspect of reading defined as word-recognition skills. (3) As a child acquires reading skills, he or she also shows improvement in auditory analysis skills. In other words, the auditory skills-reading linkup is circular. Auditory analysis skills enhance reading achievement; improved reading ability enhances auditory analysis skills. I should also mention that a similar close relationship is found between visual analysis skills and both reading comprehension and arithmetic (Rosner, 1972).

A number of other investigators have conducted studies that corroborate these conclusions. For example, Rosenberg (1980) set out to investigate the relationships between phonemic analysis skills and concrete operational thinking, and the relationships of these two in combination, with: (a) oral reading ability, (b) reading comprehension, and (c) the ability to use phonics as a word attack strategy. He used two sets of phonemic analysis skills: The Test of Auditory Analysis Skills (Rosner, 1979),[1] and the Lindamood Auditory Conceptualization Test (LAC, 1973). Among his conclusions: "(1) There is no clear cut relationship between concrete operational thinking and phonemic analysis ability; (2) phonemic analysis ability is more highly related to reading ability than is concrete operational thinking ability; (3) the TAAS was the analysis test most highly related to reading achievement; (4) the ability to pronounce words without a targeted phonemic element is the analytic task (out of the tasks employed in his study) most validly related to reading ability [p. 78]."

Slaughter (1974) carried out a similar investigation, although her main concern was to validate the hypothesis that the process of reading could be defined in three stages—letter recognition, decoding and comprehension

---

[1]The items of the TAAS are the behavioral objectives of the Auditory Skills Program of the Perceptual Skills Curriculum (Rosner, 1973), organized into the format of a norm-referenced test.

(Rosner, 1979)—and that visual and auditory perceptual skills made uniquely different contributions to each of the three. She also included a measure of listening comprehension in her study. For her perceptual skills tests she selected the Test of Visual Analysis Skills (TVAS, 1975)[2] and the TAAS. Her conclusions were also supportive. Among these: " . . . It is apparent that the three stages of reading are, in fact, significantly intercorrelated. Letter recognition (I) is relatively equally related to decoding (II), to listening comprehension (III$_L$), and to reading comprehension (III$_R$). Decoding is more closely related to reading comprehension than to listening comprehension." Further " . . . the TAAS correlates significantly with (reading stages) II, III$_R$ and III$_L$, but not with I. The TVAS explains the greatest proportion of the variance in reading comprehension (III$_R$) [p. 49]."

Yet another study worth mentioning here is one carried out by Riederer (1982), wherein she examined two questions: (1) the linkup between auditory analysis skills (as measured by the TAAS) and word recognition ability, independent of IQ differences; and (2) the relationship between binocular (vision) deficiency and reading. Her conclusions to the first: "The results indicated that the TAAS scores explained approximately 40 percent of the variance in reading scores whereas IQ accounted for only 17 percent of the variance." Hence, the children's TAAS scores represented an ability far more closely related to learning to read than did their IQ scores. Her conclusions to the second part of the study: " . . . Contrary to expectation (Riederer is a practicing optometrist), deficiencies in only two of the eight subtests of binocularity (i.e., dynamic retinoscopy and stereoacuity) occurred significantly more often in the poor reader group." " . . . the data strongly supported the first hypotheses regarding auditory analysis skills and reading, but only weakly supported the second hypothesis regarding binocular efficiency." " . . . the results of this study provided independent confirmation of some of Rosner's findings [p. 57]."

McLean (1980), a graduate student at Monash University (Melbourne, Australia), also investigated the relationship between reading achievement and auditory perception. Her study was conducted with disadvantaged grade 1 children in a Melbourne school. Her conclusions: "A statistically significant correlation was found between auditory perception (as measured by the TAAS) and reading achievement . . . supporting the value of developing the auditory perception skills of educationally disadvantaged beginning readers." McLean also cautions that "auditory perception is but one of the correlates of reading competence [p. 13]."

Weaver and Rosner (1979) used multivariate statistics to examine the relationships between visual and auditory perceptual skills on the one hand, and

---

[2]The TVAS is the counterpart to the TAAS, with the items being the objectives of the Perceptual Skills Curriculum's Visual Skills Program.

comprehension (listening and reading) that is independent of decoding (word attack skills) on the other. Once again, the results indicate what has been consistently noted above: Visual perceptual skills are linked with reading comprehension, independent of decoding; auditory analysis skills, in contrast, are related to comprehension only in that they affect the reader's word recognition abilities which, in turn, affect reading comprehension.

Finally, and extremely pertinent here, is a study conducted by Morrison (1978). He sought to (1) "... replicate, across language and culture, a 1971 study by Rosner and Simon which validated the Auditory Analysis Test (AAT) as a measure of auditory perception, highly correlated with reading achievement"; (2) "... to construct and validate a Spanish adaptation of the AAT called *La Prueba de Analisis Auditivo* (PAA) for the use with Spanish-speaking populations"; (3) "... determine the relationship between auditory analysis skills as defined by the PAA and Spanish reading performance when the effects of mental abilities are held constant"; (4) "... construct a 'validity matrix' combining the data gathered on both English and Spanish versions of the test [p. 4]."

Morrison's data supported the following conclusions: (1) "... the magnitude, direction and significance of the PAA correlations parallel those obtained by Rosner and Simon, indicating that there is a consistent relationship between auditory analysis skills as defined by the AAT and the PAA, and reading performance which is stable across differing languages, cultures and socioeconomic classes"; (2) "... auditory analysis skills in first grade Spanish reading groups are significantly related to second grade Spanish reading performance (a year later) after the effects of mental ability have been partialled out"; (3) "... significant correlations, paralleling findings reported by Rosner and Simon (1971) in their original validation study on the AAT, may shed light on the basic psycholinguistic processes that underlie reading behavior in languages with alphabetic writing systems [p. 44]." In brief, Morrison demonstrated that auditory analysis skills are closely linked to reading achievement, regardless of whether the language to be analyzed and read is English or Spanish. Given these results, it seems reasonable to argue that similar situations would be found with any group whose written language was based on sound/symbol representations.

That covers most of what I have to say about the relationship between phonoloigical awareness and reading. I want to mention only one more point, which, in turn, will lead to the second part of my talk where I will discuss some of the practical implications of all this. That point: Different reading instructional methods interact differentially with auditory analysis skills; some reading instruction programs are much more effective than others when a child's auditory analysis skills are substandard (Coleman, 1974; Rosner, 1985). Hence, it is a significant error (and the only fault I find with Bryant's efforts) to study the relationship between phonological awareness and reading without also taking into account the design of the reading instructional program that is employed.

Now to practical implications: How can knowledge of a child's phonological skills help the teacher select an effective reading instruction program? To accomplish this, I will first sketch out a rationale, then attempt to define principles for its application.

Rationale: In order to become a satisfactory (fluent and comprehending) reader, the child must be able to identify printed words, or large segments of printed words, almost instantaneously. Said differently, the child must have a great many words stored in long-term memory and be able to retrieve them with ease. To accomplish this, the child either has to invent, or be taught, a mnemonic system that reduces the burden on memory to a reasonable level, yet is based on units of analysis that are large enough to make a fluent reading possible. Surely, the best (even though not perfect) system with English words is one that exploits the connection between clusters of graphic symbols and spoken sounds.

Fortunately, most six-year-old children appear to be able to start to comprehend and use a system, given (1) adequate time (to mature and develop), (2) appropriate experiences (to acquire knowledge and the language to express that knowledge), and (3) the good luck to be born with an intact neuromotor system that enables them to exercise their innate capacity to seek order — to induce systems — in their sensory environment. Such children arrive at their first reading lesson with adequate: (1) language skills (knowledge of vocabulary, grammar, syntax); (2) understanding of the subject matter addressed in their reading texts; (3) familiarity with most of the printed letters and the conventions that govern their use; (4) awareness of the sensory units that constitute spoken words; that is, awareness of those sound units that the graphic code "codes" (thus, the reasons why testing a child's ability to analyze nonverbal stimuli does not provide relevant information).

As most experienced teachers will attest, children who enter school with these abilities could learn to read "from the telephone book"; that is, they seem to be able to learn from any reasonably organized instructional approach. They require very little extra help.

Children who lack one or more of those abilities, however, will not have such an easy time of it. The importance of the first three is evident. The child who cannot understand and speak the language, cannot comprehend the meaning of the text, or is unfamiliar with the graphic symbols, will undoubtedly encounter difficulty learning to read. The importance of the fourth ability, auditory analysis skills, is not so well recognized, but the data that both Professor Bryant and I have presented clearly illustrate that those skills are worthy of attention, that they are, indeed, significantly related to learning to read, and that the linkup is one of cause and effect.

Children who lack adequate auditory analysis skills require an instructional program that takes that deficit into account. What is adequate? How good do they have to be? The most accurate answer produces a tautology: It depends on the instructional program. A more useful answer, empirically determined, is that the term adequate auditory analysis skills, in this context, translates into the ability to delete the initial consonant sound from a spoken word (Rosner, 1973). Little surprise, therefore, in Bryant's observations about the importance of being able to detect rhyme and alliteration.

How does one go about determining the proper instructional program for children with inadequate auditory analysis skills? In general terms: (1) If the children are in kindergarten or first grade, they should engage in activities that will improve auditory analysis skills. If this is successful, and if the other abilities that were listed earlier are also at a satisfactory level, then any validated program of reading instruction should be effective. (2) If the children are in second grade or beyond and already lagging significantly in reading ability, then auditory analysis skills training will not be sufficient. For these children, the rule is: the more impaired the auditory analysis skills, the greater the need for a program that is based on phonics, a program that makes evident the close connection between phoneme and grapheme (Rosner, 1979). This, by definition, tends to rule out whole-word basal programs where the concepts of phonics are usually introduced in a relatively disorganized, often ambiguous manner, and suggests that the teacher first try an instructional approach that stresses spelling patterns (e.g., where the words to be learned at the onset are constructed mainly on such units as *at, it, in, on*). Children with substandard auditory skills must be shown (because they probably will not be able to perceive this on their own) how those words may be remembered on the basis of their shared phonetic and spelling similarities and differences, i.e., how *bit, bat, sit* and *sat* may be remembered as a related group rather than as four separate units and how remembering any one of them facilitates recall of the others. But it must also be kept in mind that children who need this kind of approach in order to perceive the system that underlies reading will probably also have to be shown how those units reoccur (and bear the same sounds) in larger, polysyllabic words, such as the *at* in spat, splatter, platitude, and so on.

Some children will not be able to grasp the underlying system even when it is exemplified by this so-called linguistic approach. For them, an even more fundamental program may be necessay, one that reveals the individual phonemic units (i.e., phonics). But, once more, simply teaching the concepts and rules of phonics will not be enough. Such children will also have to be shown how individual graphemes cluster into linguistic units, and how these, in turn, cluster into printed polysyllabic words. In other words, they must be shown, clearly and directly, how to analyze large reading units into units that they are able to identify (and give voice to) easily. Once the child has mastered the analysis task, the synthesis activity that we call reading will not be as mysterious or as dependent on rote memorization as it was before.

The probable outcomes of meeting the child's needs in this way: (1) improved word recognition skills that are derived from showing the child how to exploit what he or she already knows as a means for learning more words; (2) improved auditory analysis skills which, in turn, will improve the child's abilities to recognize cogent phonological similarities and differences in certain words, thereby reducing the need for the kind of carefully organized instruction just described.

In closing, a speculative word or two about spelling and one of the groups Professor Bryant mentioned. Given the principles just discussed, it seems reasonable to suggest that the good speller is a good speller because he or she is able to do the following: (1) Analyze spoken words into their phonemic-grapheme units, that is, display competent auditory analysis skills that enable the child to spell phonetically; (2) Invent (or learn from the teacher) the various mnemonics that make it possible to remember the spelling irregularities that pervade our language, where phonetic spelling does not work (e.g., "i before e except after c" or by voicing certain words precisely as they are spelled, as in *k*nife, ya*ch*t, etc.). Such mnemonics help the speller remember all or most of what must be memorized; all else will be spelled correctly through application of auditory analysis skills. What then explains Bryant's "good speller-poor reader" group? My speculation: They are children who depend mainly on rote memorization rather than on phonemic analysis for spelling and manage reasonably well until the word lists become too long and diverse. That, I believe, is why the "good speller-poor reader" is apt to disappear sometime during the second school year. By that time, rote memorization is not enough, and the "good speller-poor reader" becomes a "poor speller-poor reader." If what Bryant and I have presented is valid — and the available evidence is compelling — then there is no other reasonable explanation.

REFERENCES

Bruce, D. J. (1964). The analysis of word sounds by young children. *British Journal of Educational Psychology, 34,* 158–170.

Coleman, B. E. (1974). *The relationship between auditory and visual perceptual skills and first grade reading achievement under an initial phonemics-reading approach and under an initial structural linguistics reading approach.* Unpublished doctoral dissertation, University of Pittsburgh.

Koppitz, E. M. (1975). *The Bender-Gestalt test for young children.* Vols. 1 & 2. NY: Grune & Stratton.

Lindamood Auditory Conceptualization Test. (1973). Boston, MA: Teaching Resources, Inc.

McLean, P. (1980). *The relationship between reading achievement and auditory perception in disadvantaged year 1 children.* Unpublished master's thesis, Monash University, Australia.

Morrison, J. A. (1978). *La prueba de analisis auditivo: Auditory perception and Spanish reading.* Paper presented at CABE Bilingual Education Conference, Anaheim, CA.

Otis-Lennon Mental Abilities Test. (1964). NY: Harcourt, Brace and World.

Riederer, M. L. (1982). *Binocular efficiency and auditory analysis skills in good and poor readers.* Unpublished master's thesis, Simon Fraser University.

Rosenberg, S. (1980). *Phonemic analysis, concrete operations and reading an alphabetic script.* Unpublished doctoral dissertation, Hofstra University.

Rosner, J. (1969). *The design of an individualized perceptual skills curriculum,* (Working Paper #53). University of Pittsburgh, LRDC.

Rosner, J. (1971). Phonic analysis skills and beginning reading skills, *Proceedings of the American Psychological Association* (LRDC Pub #1971/9).

Rosner, J. (1972). *The development and validation of an individualized perceptual skills curriculum* (LRDC Pub. 1972/7). University of Pittsburgh, LRDC.

Rosner, J. (1973). *The perceptual skills curriculum.* NY: Walker Educational Book Corp.

Rosner, J. (1974). Auditory analysis training with prereaders. *The Reading Teacher, 27*(4), 379–384.

Rosner, J. (1979). *Helping children overcome learning difficulties* (2nd ed.). NY: Walker Publishing Co., Inc.

Rosner, J. (1985). *Perceptual skills curriculum* (2nd ed.). NY: Walker Educational Book Corp.

Rosner, J., Richman, V., & Scott, R. (1969). *The identification of children with perceptual motor dysfunction* (Working paper #47). University of Pittsburgh, LRDC.

Rosner, J., & Simon, D. (1971). The auditory analysis test: An initial report. *Journal of Learning Disabilities, 4*(7), 384–392.

Slaughter, B. A. (1974). *An examination of the relationship between a three stage process model of reading and visual and auditory perceptual skills.* Unpublished master's thesis, University of Pittsburgh.

Slosson Drawing Coordination Test. (1967). NY: Slosson Education Publishers, Inc.

Stanford Achievement Test. (1964). NY: Harcourt, Brace and World.

Starr, A. (1961). *The Rutgers Drawing Test.* Brunswick, NJ: Author.

Watkins, E. O. (1976). *The Watkins Bender-Gestalt scoring system.* San Rafael, CA: Academic Therapy.

Weaver, P., & Rosner, J. (1979). Relationship between visual and auditory perceptual skills and comprehension in students with learning disabilities. *Journal of Learning Disabilities, 12,*(9), 617–621.

5 How do Japanese Children Learn to Read?: Orthographic and Eco-cultural Variables

Giyoo Hatano
Dokkyo University, Saitama, Japan

This chapter concerns those processes through which one comes to read and write Japanese sentences fluently using knowledge of its orthography, either the standard one or one for children. The processes can be regarded as ones of spontaneous expertise resulting in the mastery of cognitive skills. This chapter gives special attention to how different the processes are from those of the English language, because of the characteristics of the Japanese orthography, and also to how similar they are in spite of the orthographic dissimilarities.

The following two omissions are to be put forward before discussing the major topics: (1) the issue of the acquisition of syntactic knowledge and vocabulary, with which orthographic knowledge interacts to enable one to read and write fluently; (2) issues related to the acquisition of paralinguistic knowledge necessary for reading comprehension — for example, how pieces of domain-specific substantive knowledge, often called schemata, and/or domain-general comprehension monitoring skills are acquired.

JAPANESE ORTHOGRAPHIES

I will state throughout this chapter that there are two orthographies in the Japanese language: the Standard Japanese Orthography (SJO) and Children's Japanese Orthography (CJO). The latter is almost always acquired in the lower grades of elementary school at the latest. Its complete acquisition prior to formal schooling is not unusual. SJO is mastered gradually through the elementary, junior high, and high school years. In other words, the two orthographies are acquired with roughly 10 years of horizontal decalage. I will describe both orthographies briefly so that readers can better understand discussions in the following sections.

Standard Japanese Orthography (SJO)

Standard Japanese sentences in newspapers, books, journals, and letters are written by using both Chinese characters (kanji) and hiragana, one of the two kinds of kana syllabaries (See b in Figure 5.1). The SJO sentences, written from top to bottom, or from left to right, are separated by two kinds of punctuation marks, roughly corresponding to the comma and period in English, but words are not separated from one another. Thus, the very first task for a reader after recognizing letters is to segment the string of letters between the punctuation marks into a sequence of words or sentence segments. There are several rules-of-thumb governing whether a word is written in kana or kanji. Particles are always written in kana. Auxiliary verbs are written in kana in most cases. Nouns and verb/adjective stems are usually written in kanji, while inflections are written in kana. Thus, for an experienced reader, it is fairly easy to divide a sentence written in a combination of kanji and kana into words or sentence segments and to parse it syntactically. This is probably the main reason why words and sentence segments are not written separately in standard Japanese sentences.

Hiragana are 71 simple-figured characters, each representing one syllable (with minor exceptions described below)—the correspondence is nearly one-to-one. Of the 71, 25 representing voiced and semi-voiced sounds are made of the corresponding unvoiced sound characters and special marks for voiced/

a) The Japanese cognitive science society was established in 1983. Profession Toda

was elected as its first president.

b) 日本認知科学会は. 1983年に. 設立された.
戸田教授が. その初代会長に選出された.

c) にほんにんちかがくかいは. 1983ねんに
せつりつされた. とだきょうじゅが その
しょだいかいちょうに. せんしゅつされた.

d) Nihonninchikagakkaiwa 1983nenni setsuritsusareta. Todakyojuga sono shodaikaichoni

senshutsusareta.

FIG. 5.1   Japanese sentences written in the standard Japanese orthography (b), in *hiragana* (c), in English alphabet letters (d), and the corresponding English sentence (a).

semi-voiced. Therefore, there are only 46 basic kana characters. Kanji, the Chinese characters, represent morphemes. They usually have a prototypal meaning and unique but multiple pronunciations, sometimes consisting of multiple syllables. In Japan, about 2000 kanji are designated as kanji for daily use, and about half are taught in elementary school. In addition to kanji and hiragana, katakana and Arabic numerals are also used in Japanese sentences. Katakana, again 71 characters, are used to represent words of foreign origin and onomatopoeic expression.

A few comments on both of the major scripts might be added here. Although in the Japanese language the number of kinds of syllables is limited because consonants never occur consecutively, the 71 kana are not sufficient. There are five types of special syllables — long syllables, contracted ones, contracted long ones, assimilated ones and the syllabic nasal. These special syllables are expressed by two or three kana, and a special kana is used for the last one exclusively. To depict contracted and assimilated syllables with two kana, the second is made smaller so that they can easily be distinguished from two consecutive ordinary syllables. Furthermore, exceptions exist for three kana representing case participles: two of them are pronounced differently when they represent case particles, and the third one is used exclusively for a case particle and shares the same pronunciation as another kana used for ordinary words. Therefore, the script-sound correspondence of kana is not perfect, as is often asserted.

A unique characteristic of kanji in the Japanese language, not shared by Chinese characters in the Chinese or Korean language, is that most of them are given a Japanese and a Chinese reading (i.e., two pronunciations, each having the same meaning). Each Japanese reading was historically originated by attaching to a Chinese character a native Japanese word representing the meaning of the character. Therefore, the Japanese reading is sometimes called the semantic reading, while the Chinese reading is regarded as the phonetic reading. A rough approximation in English is found in "etc.": "et cetera" could be called the Latin reading and "and so on" the English reading.

The Chinese and Japanese readings are usually quite dissimilar. For example, the Chinese reading for 水 is *sui,* while its Japanese reading is *mizu.* However, irrespective of the reading chosen, the character has the core, prototypal meaning of "water," which may be expanded to such other meanings as sea, flood, or moisture when combined with other kanji. Some kanji have several different meanings in the Japanese language and thus several Japanese readings. Other kanji have several different Chinese readings because of the historical changes of their pronunciation. For example, 生 has six Japanese readings and two Chinese ones. However, when a kanji is combined with other kanji or kana to make a compound word or derivative, only one reading is usually given. For example, 生 in 生活費 (cost of living) is always read *sei* (one of the Chinese readings), while the same character in 生卵 (raw egg) is read *nama* (a Japanese reading).

Since the Japanese language has many fewer kinds of syllables and less clear intonation or accent differences than the Chinese language, many kanji must share one and the same Chinese reading. For example, more than 70 of the 2000 kanji used everyday have the Chinese reading of *ko*. But these 70 homonyms are differentiated by unique kanji.

In sum, there is a many-to-many correspondence between a kanji and its readings. This is not the case for Chinese characters in Chinese, where each character is always given one and the same reading, shared by few, if any, other characters.

Children's Japanese Orthography (CJO)

Japanese sentences in picture books and magazines for preschool and grade K[1] children are written by using hiragana and Arabic numerals. When the target audience is lower grade children, katakana and a small number of kanji are added. However, those kanji are usually accompanied by hiragana, called furigana, which show their pronunciation.

In these materials, sentences are divided into sentence segments by placing some space before each "substantive" word. Therefore, by knowing hiragana, one can easily read every sentence. CJO requires learning a few processing rules for special syllables and case particles in addition to the "regular" script-sound correspondences for the ordinary syllables. The fact that CJO materials are available to Japanese children seems to be the main reason why it is believed that learning to read is very easy in Japanese.

When sentences are written in CJO, difficult, "adult" kanji compound words are avoided. Naturally, words appearing in CJO materials are mostly within children's vocabulary and are familiar when pronounced. More and more kanji are added, as those expected to read them grow older.

KANA-KANJI DIFFERENCES IN VISUAL WORD RECOGNITION AND TRANSCRIPTION

Retrievability Relationships Among Various Internal Codes of a Word

We Japanese think that giving each kanji a Japanese reading in addition to its Chinese reading has strengthened the association between that kanji and

---

[1] Japanese kindergartens usually include 4-year-olds and sometimes 3-year-olds and are not regarded as part of the elementary school. For the convenience of American readers, I use this term to refer to the year just preceding grade 1.

its meaning. At the same time, this dual "reading" system has weakened the association between a kanji and either of its readings, as has the fact that many kanji share the same Chinese reading.

Does this unique characteristic of the dual readings of kanji affect the information-processing of words in the Japanese language? I think YES. Many substantive words in Japanese comprise several kanji, with or without kana. They are given either the Japanese or Chinese reading, seldom both. Among them, almost all western-originated technical terms are kanji compound words with the Chinese reading. However, because of the strengthened association of the component kanji with meaning and of the weakened association with pronunciation as described above, I assume that the meanings of words transcribed in kanji can readily be retrieved without being mediated by phonetic codes.

I take for granted that an "ordinary" experienced reader of Japanese utilizes in reading and writing four different internal codes for a word. Retrievability relationships among them are shown schematically in the model in Figure 5.2. (This model should not be interpreted as indicating processing strategies for reading and writing.) Two of the codes are kanji and kana, usually in the form of the visual image of the component characters. The third is the phonetic code, which is the auditory image of pronunciation. The last code is the "meaning," a set of knowledge about the referent of the word (e.g., its appearance, definition, functions, contexts of use, etc.). All these codes except for the kana code, which is directly interchangeable with the phonetic code, are supposedly registered under each entry in the mental lexicon when it is fully developed. Therefore, as the broken line in Figure 5.2 suggests, any code can retrieve any other by referring to the mental lexicon as long as the target word is contained in it. However, some relationships among the codes are direct, and one code can retrieve another without referring to the lexicon. The kana-to-phonetic code transfer or phonetic-to-kana code transfer is usually readily accomplished and is almost always possible, either by the script-sound correspondence rule or phonetic analogy, even when a given string of sounds or symbols does not constitute a known word. Thus, these two codes are connected by a bold line in Figure 5.2. The prelexical retrieval of the phonetic code from the kanji can also often be done, though there is sometimes more than one possible correspondence. For example, experienced readers of Japanese can pronounce, though tentatively, 検索 (retrieval) as *kensaku,* even when they have never seen this combination of kanji. In addition, the kanji code can often induce meaning directly as mentioned above. Moreover, even though retrieval of kanji from the phonetic code cannot be done directly in most cases because there are many kanji corresponding to a given phonetic code, a combination of the phonetic and meaning codes determine the kanji code (see pair of half arrowheads pointing towards kanji code in Figure 5.2). As will be discussed in more detail

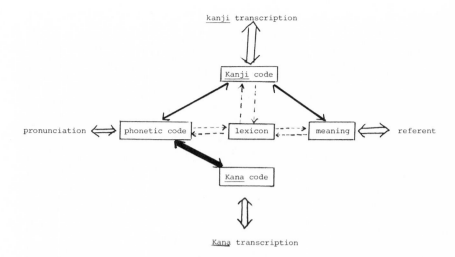

FIG. 5.2   Retrievability relationships among mental lexicon, various internal codes of a word, and the corresponding observables.

later, this combination of codes can determine the kanji code even when the target word does not exist among the lexical entries.

The assumed retrievability relationships schematized in Figure 5.2 have been supported by the following two streams of research: observations of kana-kanji selective impairments among aphasic and alexic patients, and laboratory experiments on processing of the two types of characters. Let me summarize their major findings.

Studies with Aphasic and Alexic Patients

Some aphasic and alexic patients perform much better with kanji than kana. Alexic patients without agraphia provide the clearest example. It is generally agreed that for them the visual image of script cannot directly produce an auditory image of the word. In other words, neither the kana nor the kanji code can directly be transformed into the phonetic code by them. Shortly after the causal injury, such patients cannot read or comprehend words written in kana, although their performance can be improved after practicing such "motor mediation" as tracing a character with a finger. Without such remediation, they often can read kanji, even complex and difficult ones that most elementary school children do not know. Even when they cannot read words transcribed in kanji, they can generate "pregestalt" responses. That is, they can state such things as where and when the referent of the word is used and what it is like (Iwata, 1976). This strongly suggests, at least for those patients, that there is a direct path from the kanji code to the meaning, through which the phonetic code is retrieved; the disconnection between the kana code and the phonetic code makes the former isolated from other codes and useless.

Aphasic patients with apraxia also tend to perform better with kanji than kana. In this type of aphasia the function of phonetic articulation is injured. As a result, the phonetic code of a word is very unstable, and only with difficulty can patients retrieve from it the kana code or meaning. For them, writing a word in kana corresponding to the object shown, a task presumably mediated by the phonetic code, is much harder than writing in kanji, a task not involving phonetic mediation. Such patients also tend to have greater difficulty with kana than kanji in a word-naming task when the word is shown by a tachistoscope for a short duration. Sasanuma and Fujimura (1971) presented clear evidence for the difficulty in kana transcription and recognition. Interestingly, the aphasic patients with apraxia retained what they acquired later (i.e., kanji) much better than what they had acquired earlier (i.e., kana). For simple aphasic patients the reverse was true. They processed kana transcription more accurately than kanji transcription.

On the other hand, there is a small number of patients of aphasia, originally named by Imura (1943) as the "word meaning" aphasia, who show greater difficulty in reading and writing kanji than kana. Such patients can repeat a given word or sentence, but cannot comprehend its meaning. According to the model in Figure 5.2, they fail to retrieve the meaning from either the phonetic code or the kanji code. Thus, they can read kana transcription correctly though monotonously but sometimes cannot choose the appropriate reading for the kanji transcription. Sasanuma and Monoi (1975) reported that such aphasic subjects could give names in correct kana transcription to everyday objects but failed to do so in most cases in kanji transcription. The patients gave a combination of kanji that were phonetically equivalent to the target word, but semantically incompatible with the context. The phonetic code alone cannot determine how to write the word in kanji transcription. The meaning must take part in it.

Laboratory Studies on the Processing of Kana and Kanji

The following two experimental studies are directly relevant to the model depicted in Figure 5.2. Umemura (1981), choosing 50 frequently used kanji characters, half with one syllable and half with two syllables, measured the time necessary to read aloud lists consisting of these characters and their kana transcriptions. College students were required to read one of the lists as fast as possible. Those assigned to the kanji lists were told that they would be given kanji of one or two syllables. Umemura found that the reading rate was faster for the kana than for the kanji list, and that there was no difference in the reading rate between the one-syllable and two-syllable kanji list because the latter were read twice as fast as the former. The first finding is consistent with the model, predicting faster retrieval of the phonetic code from the kana than from the kanji code. The last finding may mean that phonetic coding of kanji tends to chunk phonemes (i.e., syllables) in terms of semantic units.

Saito (1981) reported two of his experiments, one extending the above findings and the other introducing semantic congruence judgments. In the first experiment, native Japanese subjects were presented stimulus words, in either kana or kanji, and required to read aloud as quickly as possible. The words varied in the number of morae (i.e., syllables or units of metrical time) they contained. The results revealed that kana were read aloud more rapidly than kanji, corroborating the findings of Umemura (1981). The results also showed that oral reading time for kanji was not affected by the number of syllables pronounced, while for kana it was.

In the second experiment, subjects were presented a target word and a sentence containing it and required to judge whether the word was semantically congruent with the sentence. When subjects were allowed to read silently, kanji words were judged for semantic appropriateness faster than kana words. When asked to read aloud, subjects showed no difference in the speed of judgment. Thus, Saito concludes that in the silent reading condition kanji words are processed directly from visual form (i.e., graphemic codes) to meaning (i.e., semantic codes), whereas the processing of kana words from graphemic code to meaning is mediated through the sound system. However, kanji words present some difficulties for reading aloud with the appropriate pronunciation.

Parallel findings are expected for kana and kanji word transcription. I predict: (1) When a familiar object is shown, or its name is given orally, there will be longer latency for generating kanji transcription than kana transcription, and (2) although the latency for kana transcription will increase with the number of syllables (or morae), the latency will be nearly constant for kanji across different numbers of syllables, the number of strokes being controlled. So far, there have been no empirical studies examining these predictions.

EXPERTS' USE OF KANJI IN READING

As Glushko (1979) aptly pointed out, an orthography has many different goals, and its desirability varies between readers and writers and according to the extent of their expertise. The use of the basic 2000 kanji is apt to be inhibitory for beginners, in either reading or writing. In fact, Japanese students have to spend much time acquiring SJO, especially learning how to read and write kanji. For experienced writers, the use of kanji is not a big problem, except for the inconvenience of typing. (Until the very recent development of a word processor for Japanese, typewriting of Japanese sentences had seldom been done except by professional typists.) Therefore, SJO may benefit experienced readers only. It allows readers to comprehend a text faster and more easily, because the use of kanji makes segmentation clearer and parsing more straightforward. According to Kitao (1960), compared with the corresponding hiragana-only transcription, college students read the kanji-kana combined transcription 15% faster and as measured by the cloze procedure, comprehended 10% better. Of course, this observed superiority should be considered in light of the subjects' familiarity with the kanji-kana combined transcription.

Suzuki (1975, 1977) claimed that kanji help readers resolve homonymic ambiguity and infer meanings of unfamiliar words. I believe that, if we can empirically demonstrate these "functions" of kanji to exist, we can give reasonable answers to such questions often asked by foreigners as well as by "reformers" of the Japanese orthography as: "Is the use of kanji really necessary?", "Aren't kanji preserved only because of the cultural tradition?", "Do all Japanese have to spend so much time acquiring SJO when CJO seems sufficient for reading and writing Japanese?" Now let me describe several experiments in which my associates and I have examined these functions.

Kanji's Function: Resolution of Homonymic Ambiguity

An experiment by Kuhara and Hatano (1981) with college students, though intended to investigate the effects of headings on discourse comprehension, clearly shows how useful kanji are for eliminating homonymic confusion. Passages given orally included an "ambiguous" target word, the meaning of which was often mistaken for that of its homonym. More specifically, the passages, an example of which is shown in Figure 5.3, were constructed as follows: The first part of each passage included an ambiguous target word (e.g., 荒天 — rough weather, read *kouten*), which was less readily retrievable than its homonym (好天 — good weather, also read *kouten*). When a group of students were asked to change the kana-written target words into kanji, only 18% of the responses were the target word (e.g., 荒天), whereas 79% were the homonyms (好天). The last sentence included the target word in an unambiguous context to facilitate correct comprehension of the passage. (In fact, with the ambiguity thus removed, another group of students changed the kana-written target words into the correct kanji much more easily, though the proportion of target responses still varied depending on the clarity of disambiguation: 87% for the two passages in which the context had the strongest effects, and 25% for the two passages in which the context effects were the weakest.)

When listeners encode the target word incorrectly and find that its meaning is inconsistent with the postcontextual information, they not only have to change the encoding but also reconstruct the entire picture from the passage. This "backward" processing may not be successful and may require much in-

| Target word: | kouten | Target response is "rough weather." |
| | | Homonym response is "good weather." |

Heading: Forecast of continuing bad weather.

Passage: 1.   Physical education teaching assistant Moriyama is now trying to climb the IV summit of Annapurna in the Himalayas as a member of the university alpinists joint expedition.

2.   (critical sentence)

According to the most recent report to the editors of the News:

The weather forecast on the morning of the 5th said that kouten would continue for several days, creating a tense situation in the 5th camp.

3.   In the Himalayas, there is usually a major change in the weather every several days.

4.   Success or failure depends on how well one manages to endure stormy days and take advantage of calm days.

5.   (post-contextual sentence)

If there is no accident during the several days of kouten, it is possible to conquer the summit after the weather improves.

Comprehension test:

According to the weather forecast, the several days that followed the 5th would be fine.   (FALSE)

FIG. 5.3   An example of the news passage (weak context).

formation processing. Therefore, giving a heading before listening to the passage makes this cumbersome backward processing unnecessary and enhances comprehension.

Two experimental groups were given written kanji headings and synonym headings, respectively. The kanji heading included a target word transcribed in kanji. The synonym heading included a synonym for the target word, also transcribed in kanji. In addition to giving context for comprehension of the passage, the kanji heading gave direct encoding cues for the target word, whereas the synonym heading gave only indirect ones, because it did not share component kanji with the target word. The control, no-heading group simply had a "station break" saying "next news" between the passages.

All the students were asked to listen to the narration of ten news passages with headings or station breaks and to memorize the target words and the substance of the passages. Each target word was presented visually with a signal bell sound. Except for the kanji headings, the target words were transcribed in kana for all the groups. Then the students were given the following paper-and-pencil tests: (1) a comprehension test of the news passages, asking the subject to judge whether each of the sentences, which were substantively consistent either with the meaning of the target word or its homonym, was true or false; and (2) a test of kanji encoding, asking them to change the kana-transcribed target words in the ambiguous context into kanji.

Table 5.1 shows the mean proportions of correct responses on the comprehension test and of the target and the homonym responses on the kanji encoding test. A one–way analysis of variance (ANOVA) on the number of correct responses on the comprehension test revealed a highly significant group effect. Both the kanji and the synonym-heading groups had a significantly greater number of correct responses than the no-heading group. Also, the kanji-heading group had slightly, though significantly, more correct responses than the synonym-heading group.

One-way ANOVAs performed on the numbers of the target and the homonym responses on the kanji encoding test showed significant group effects. The kanji–heading group had many more target (i.e., correct) responses and fewer homonym (i.e., incorrect) responses than the other two groups, and the synonym-heading group produced a few more target responses and fewer homonym responses than the no-heading group. All these differences were significant. As for the kanji-heading group, the difference in encoding between target responses to the strong and weak context passages was slight (91% and 85%), whereas there were large differences in the synonym- (51% and 5%) and the no-heading group (22% and 6%).

These results suggest that, although either heading gives a proper context for interpretation and greatly facilitates comprehension of the passage as a whole, only the kanji heading does so for the correct encoding of the target word. In other words, kanji can completely solve homonymic ambiguity.

TABLE 5.1
The Mean Proportions of Correct Responses on the Comprehension
Test and the Target/Homonym Responses on the *Kanji* Encoding Test

	Comprehension	Kanji Encoding	
Group	*Correct*	*Target*	*Homonym*
Kanji-heading	.78	.88	.10
Synonym-heading	.72	.33	.56
No-heading	.51	.18	.75

Kanji's Function: High Inferability of Meaning of Unfamiliar Words

Now let us turn to our experiments on the function of kanji in inferring the meanings of unfamiliar words, more specifically technical terms (Hatano, Kuhara, & Akiyama, 1981). In the Japanese language most technical terms, which are often translations from one of the European languages, are made up of two or more kanji. The resulting compound is usually given a Chinese reading, which is simply the Chinese readings in order of the component kanji. This seems similar to the practice in English of combining Greek or Latin words. In both cases, these are compound words consisting of morphemes that are not used in daily conversation and are free from varieties of connotations, but are semantically appropriate. The model in Figure 5.2 implies that technical terms transcribed in kanji are better understood than the corresponding kana transcriptions and also, though implicitly, are better understood than Greek- or Latin-derived compound words in English.[2] This prediction was initially made by Suzuki (1975). He gave two primary reasons: (1) The component kanji are semantically understood far more easily than the component Greek or Latin words, because the former are already imbued with Japanese or semantic readings. (2) The component kanji, unlike Greek or Latin components, are not deformed by the influence of modified pronunciation. For example, the meaning of 白血病 (*hakketsubyō*) is much more easily inferred than that of *leukemia*. Each component kanji is given a Japanese reading, *shiroi* (white), *chi* (blood), and *yamai* (disease), respectively. The first two Japanese readings are easily understood even by preschool children. The last one is a little old-fashioned, but young children know it as *byo* of *byoki* (disease). Thus, though it is impossible to understand intuitively its exact nature, readers of Japanese can infer that the word means "a disease that turns blood white." The English word can be divided into "leuk(o)," "hem(o)," and "ia," but the first two Greek-origin morphemes are not easily understood by the uneducated, I think, because they do not have semantic readings. Moreover, readers of English may fail to identify "hem(o)" in leukemia because of the spelling change.

In our experiment, undergraduates were asked to match 30 unfamiliar, technical terms with their definitions, descriptions, or both. We selected 30 Latin or Greek-derived English technical terms and their Japanese translations, which were kanji compound words with two to five component characters from a list compiled by Suzuki (1978). The terms were mostly from bot-

---

[2]It may be possible to access the entry in the mental lexicon from the alphabetical code directly, without mediation by the phonetic code (see Kleiman, 1975), but this does not mean that the alphabetical code induces the meaning more promptly than the phonetic code. Moreover, the direct access would be limited to the case where an experienced reader processes a familiar word.

any, zoology, medical science, psychology or linguistics. Two examples of the technical terms and their definitions are: *limnology*—the scientific study of physical, chemical, and biological conditions in lakes and ponds—and *piscivorous*—eating fish as a regular diet.

Three groups of Japanese students were asked to match the words with their definitions in Japanese. The word lists were presented in kanji, kana, and English, respectively. A group of American students were tested by using the English definitions and word list. The results are shown in Figure 5.4. The inferability in the kanji condition was almost perfect. Why was it so easy to

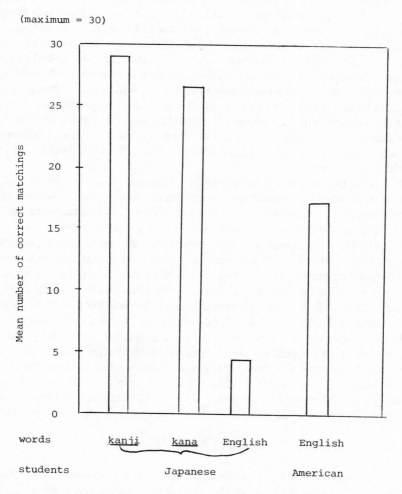

FIG. 5.4   Mean number of correct matchings of definitions with words.

infer meanings from the kanji expressions? The kanji expression for limnology is constructed of three characters, 湖沼学. These three characters have semantic readings roughly corresponding to "lake(s)," "pond(s)," and "study (studies)," respectively, and these semantic readings can easily be understood even by children. Similarly, the component kanji of the Japanese word corresponding to "piscivorous" are literally "fish-eat-nature."

The order of performance of the four conditions was kanji, kana, English/American students and English/Japanese students. It is not surprising that the Japanese students in the English condition performed poorest, because English was not their first language. The kanji condition was superior to any other condition. This is consistent with our prediction that the words in kanji have higher inferability than the words in kana and English. Another interpretation is possible, however: Japanese students are already more familiar than Americans with the technical terms. To check this, we asked other groups of Japanese and American students to write the words corresponding to the 30 definitions. When the students did not know the word, they were encouraged to invent them. The mean number of correct responses, which included inventions, was 7.23 for the Japanese students and 5.00 for the American students. The difference in mean number of correct responses between the two groups was small, and could not explain the large difference in matching performance.

The reader may wonder if meanings of component kanji are really sufficient cues for inferring the meaning of most compound words. It is true that the meaning of a compound word, even an artificially constructed word like a technical term, cannot be determined solely by the meanings of its component kanji. However, there are other constraints on the range of possible meanings for the word. First, experienced readers have acquired several compounding schemata by which kanji words are constructed. For example, when two nouns are compounded, the new word belongs to a family of the last noun. Thus, 乳牛 (milk-cow) means a cow for milking and 牛乳 (cow-milk) means milk of a cow. Second, our world knowledge can be used to exclude some possible meanings and also to choose other, more likely ones. This is similar to English speakers' differentiated interpretation of structurally similar phrases like "horseshoe" and "alligator shoe." Finally, the context of the sentence, passage, or work as a whole can give additional clues to the meaning of the word in question. Therefore, meanings of component kanji only increase the inferability, but this increment is often very helpful.

The Latent Cognitive Function of Kanji

As we see from Figure 5.4, the undergraduates in the previous experiment matched kana-transcribed, unfamiliar technical terms with definitions fairly well. The performance in the kana condition was only a little lower than that in the kanji condition. I assume that this is because students in the kana condition, by using the definitions as contextual information, often succeeded in retrieving the appropriate kanji that satisfied the phonetic constraint of the kana and then utilized the kanji to infer the meaning. Following the model in Figure 5.2, a series of transformations, starting with the kana code and moving through the phonetic code and the kanji code, induced the meaning.

Of course, there are many possible kanji codes that satisfy the phonetic constraint, and a subject may have to try a number of combinations of component kanji. Take *gyoshokusei*, for example. According to the Iwanami dictionary of Japanese, there are three characters read *gyo*, ten read *shoku* and 33 read *sei*. Therefore, even when the phonetic code is correctly segmented, there are 990 possible combinations of kanji to examine. However, in the case of *gyo*, one of the three characters (i.e., 魚) is salient because its Japanese reading (i.e., *sakana*, fish) appears in one of the 30 definitions. (For the other two characters *gyo*, no Japanese readings appear in the definitions.) Thus, the number of likely candidates is nowhere near 990.

In summary, even when the apparent task for the reader is to infer the meaning from the kana transcription, the kanji code is used as a mediator. Thus, kanji apparently have a latent cognitive function.

If we were right in concluding that the subjects' inferring the meaning was mediated by the kanji code, then the correctness or incorrectness of the inferred meaning would depend upon their finding the correct kanji. To test this, we examined the kanji representation of the technical terms chosen by the students in the kana condition. After matching the definitions with the words, the students in the kana condition were given a kanji encoding test. In the test, they were given the correct combinations of 30 definitions and corresponding kana words and were asked to change the kana into kanji. We examined the proportion of correct matchings of the definitions with the words as a function of correctness in this kanji encoding test. When kanji encodings were correct, the mean proportion of the correct matching was 0.89; but when kanji encoding responses were incorrect or missing, the mean proportion was 0.69.

This difference is statistically significant, but the latter proportion is still fairly high. This is almost certainly due to the fact that one must get only the critical character(s) correct in order to make the correct matching. For example, the Japanese word corresponding to "laryingal" consists of three kanji, but only the last one, meaning "sound," is critical to matching the word with the definition, "a sound articulated between vocal cords when breathing out."

We conducted the second experiment to examine the correspondence of inferred meanings and the kanji representation of technical terms in a weaker sentential context. Ten technical terms sampled from the main experiment were used. Each of the sentences included one target word written in kana and underlined. As shown in the following examples, the target words were not given strong sentence contexts, as had the definitions in the main experiment: (1) he is a specialist in *koshōgaku* (limnology) and has studied everywhere in Japan; (2) this animal lives by the river bank and is *gyoshokusei* (piscivorous).

A group of Japanese undergraduates were asked to write the meanings of the kana target words and, after this test sheet was collected, to change the target words into kanji. Both inferred meanings and kanji encodings were classified into three categories: correct response; incorrect response, and no-answer, including incomplete response. The relationships between the meanings and kanji encodings were examined. The correspondence between inferred meanings and kanji encodings was very close, as we can see in Table 5.2. When the students made correct kanji encodings, they inferred correct meanings in most cases. When they retrieved incorrect kanji, inferred meanings were also incorrect. Where the students failed to give kanji, they could not infer meanings.

Close correspondence was observed also within the incorrect responses. Three different incorrect responses were given for *koshōgaku* (i.e., limnology) in the kanji encoding test: 古証学, 古匹学 and 古杓学, all *koshōgaku* in pronunciation. The component kanji have the meanings of "old-document-study," "old-artist-study" and "old-naming-study," respectively. As expected, the meanings of the word inferred by the students are highly similar to the integration of the meanings of the three component kanji. For example, students who gave 古匹学 in the kanji encoding test inferred that *koshōgaku* was a study of great artists in old days. There were few incorrect responses for *gyoshokusei* (i.e., piscivorous). This can be attributed in part to the small number of kanji having the pronunciation "gyo."

Kanji Code in the Process of Inferring Meaning

The second experiment just described clearly showed the close correspondence between inferred meanings and kanji encodings. However, we cannot claim from this alone that the kanji code was used as a mediator in inferring

TABLE 5.2
Relationships Between Meaning and *Kanji* Encoding
of Target Words

Meaning	Kanji Responses		
	Correct	Incorrect	No answer
Correct	51.2%	4.2%	0.8%
Incorrect	2.7	16.9	1.5
No answer	6.5	6.2	10.0

the meaning. A rival interpretation is that, using contextual information, the subject first guessed the meaning of an unfamiliar word and then assigned kanji that would constitute a semantically corresponding combination. Another likely interpretation is that, though the target words were unfamiliar without proper context, their meanings could be retrieved from the mental lexicon with the appropriate contextual help.

To examine these interpretations, we (Kojima and Hatano, in preparation-a) conducted another experiment in which college students were individually asked to guess, and then to choose from among alternatives, the meaning of an unfamiliar word and to verbalize, as much as possible, the process of inferring. The corresponding English words, as well as the ten Japanese kanji compound words, were embedded in contextual sentences similar to those used in the second experiment. Finally, the subject was asked about his or her general strategy for figuring out the meaning, such as what cues had been used in the preceding phase. The experimenter carefully avoided suggesting the subject use or refer to kanji.

Of the 23 college students experimentally given kanji compound words, 22 replied, when asked about their general strategy, that they had used kanji in inferring the meaning. All 23 spontaneously referred at least once to kanji with verbalizations like "...if I change it into kanji...," "...to assign kanji..." For the ten items, such spontaneous reference to kanji occurred 45%.

The subjects often stated that they could not figure out the meaning because they could not think of appropriate kanji. The following are a few examples:

(Taperecorder: "*Koshōgaku.* He is a specialist in *koshogaku* and has studied everywhere in Japan. (Subject's verbalization:) *Koshogaku*—a name of a science—because *gaku* is attached last—this must be the *gaku* of *gakumon*—I thought this by trying to imagine the kanji—but I don't know what *koshō* is.

(Taperecorder:) *Tōsokurui.* There are many foreigners who reject *toso-kurui,* although they can eat shellfish. (Subject's verbalization:) *Soku* may be *ashi* (the Japanese reading meaning foot or feet)—I cannot figure out what *to* means—I guess the word means a living thing with feet."

When subjects selected incorrect kanji that shared the same pronunciation, they usually guessed the corresponding incorrect meaning, as the second experiment had suggested. Moreover, in the second phase of the experiment, where subjects were asked to choose the correct meaning of four alternatives given orally, they tended to choose a different meaning from the one they had guessed in the first phase, when they thought of another kanji while examining the alternatives.

The subjects' guessing and choosing the meaning of unfamiliar words were strongly constrained by the need for the kanji to satisfy the phonetic code.

Compared with subjects tested with the English words, the subjects tested with the kanji compound words not only made many more correct responses but also generated a much more limited range of erroneous responses.

Similar experimental procedures were applied to five blind college students who had not learned to read or write kanji. (Japanese braille is limited to syllabaries.) Unexpectedly, four of them almost always referred to kanji spontaneously. Even though they did not know the configuration of the kanji whose Chinese reading was *sui* (水), they did know it had another reading, *mizu,* and had the prototypal meaning of water. Since the standard Japanese orthography (SJO) constitutes an integral part of the Japanese culture, even the blind, in order to be successful in the academic world, have to learn multiple readings of kanji and use that knowledge in inferring the meaning of unfamiliar words, although their kanji codes are purely propositional.

Unlike the blind, the sighted should acquire a figurative form of the kanji code. If so, we can predict that, when sighted subjects try to use the kanji code, a concurrent or preloaded visuo-spatial task would be more damaging than an aural-verbal one, whereas the reverse would be true when they use the kana or phonetic code (see Brooks, 1967; Baddeley & Lieberman, 1980). We are now testing this prediction.

In summary, these experiments demonstrate kanji's latent cognitive functions. Experienced readers of Japanese try to find a combination of kanji satisfying the given phonetic code of kana transcription that seems to be appropriate in the context, and then they infer the meaning. (They can be expected to rely on a similar procedure when a pronounced word is ambiguous because of the presence of homonyms.) This is the opposite of what has been demonstrated by several psycholinguistic studies (e.g., Rubenstein, Lewis, & Rubenstein, 1971), where a word written in English is transformed into a phonetic code before its meaning is retrieved. Such phonetic transformation may be true with the Japanese language provided the word is written in kana and is a familiar one.

That kanji have such latent cognitive functions has an important implication. Readers of Japanese can understand unfamiliar words, spoken or in kana, with the help of kanji codes stored in long term memory. Therefore, it may well be misleading to claim that the use of kanji can be reduced without much sacrifice because readers of Japanese can communicate effectively in the spoken language.

ACQUISITION OF CJO

As mentioned earlier, by the time they reach the lower grades in elementary school, most children born in Japanese-speaking homes acquire the children's Japanese orthography (CJO) and can fluently read books for children.

Children who are greatly interested in reading become CJO experts as early as their fourth birthday. Let me describe my own observation of a 4.1-year-old boy, a nephew of a colleague of mine, as a concrete example of a CJO expert. This little boy, though born in a middle-class family and brighter than average, is not an especially gifted child. First, when a sentence consisted of words within his vocabulary and was written in CJO, he could read the sentence fluently at the first attempt and comprehend the meaning, as revealed by his answers to simple questions and paraphrasing. The special syllables and specially pronounced case particles did not disturb him at all. Second, when a sentence involved some unfamiliar words, he skipped them at first but then read them rather smoothly, in word-like fashion, at the second attempt. Third, when a sentence was not divided into segments, as is done in CJO, he had only slight trouble in segmentation. Fourth, at the first attempt he could read aloud fairly smoothly syntactically erroneous sentences. Fifth, when he was asked to read false sentences, he showed various forms of resistance. This means that he understood the meaning, at least roughly, before reading the sentences aloud. For example, he refused to read the predicate of the sentence, "K-obasan ("Aunt" K, the experimenter) has three eyes." He read reluctantly, "K-obasan is sleeping," but added the expression, "this says." He changed the sentence, "M-kun (his name) is a girl" into "M-kun is a boy," at the first attempt and asked the experimenter to correct it, "because it was false." Finally, he could read most katakana and at least 30 kanji.

How Well Can Young Children Read? — Surveys of the NLRI of Japan

This little boy is more advanced than most of his agemates, but he is not a rare exception; the majority of his agemates will also become CJO experts in a couple of years. This is suggested by nationwide surveys conducted in 1967 by Muraishi and Amano at the National Language Research Institute (NLRI) of Japan, and by other small-scale surveys showing further acceleration of CJO acquisition (see a review by Muraishi, 1971).

Figure 5.5 shows the shape of the distribution of the number of kana characters, out of a total of 71, that grade K children could read. The distribution is J-shaped: A majority of the children could read most of the kana characters. The distribution is U-shaped for children one year younger: There are many children who could read most kana characters, many who could read almost none, and a small number in between. As the investigators pointed out, the speed of acquisition of kana reading is slow initially but accelerates greatly after about 20 characters are mastered.

The above result does not guarantee that many of the tested children could read the special syllables or case particles. Only 20% of the children one year younger than grade K could read correctly the two special case particles (i.e.,

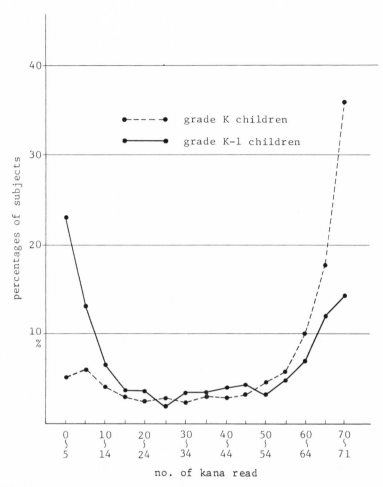

FIG. 5.5   Distribution of number of kana characters read by young children (maximum = 71) (from NLRI, 1972).

ha for *wa* and *he* for *e*). The figures were even lower for the special syllables. Among those, special syllables, contracted syllables, and contracted long syllables were especially difficult to read. For example, these young children often failed to read a sequence of three kana, *shi-yo-u,* as a contracted long syllable, *shyō*. At grade K, the corresponding figures for the two special case particles were a little higher: 50% and 30% for the girls, and a little lower for boys. Only 9% of the girls and 6% of the boys could read all the special syllables and case particles.

The NLRI study clearly demonstrates the order of sequence in learning to read kana characters. First, children acquire the ability to read basic kana (i.e., 46 kana characters representing 44 unvoiced sounds, a case particle and the syllabic nasal). Next, they acquire the ability to read all other kana for voiced and half-voiced sounds, which are made by adding one of the two special marks to the basic kana. In other words, they can now read all of the 71 kana for ordinary syllables. Finally, they learn how to read the two specially pronounced case particles and four special syllables in which two or three kana are combined to represent those syllables.

It will be interesting to compare Japanese children's reading and writing ability with that of American children. The Hess-Azuma study on cognitive socialization (Azuma, Kashiwagi & Hess, 1981) included relevant data, controlling for socio-economic status. Five-year-old Japanese children living in Tokyo or Sapporo were asked to name kana characters including several voiced ones; five-year-old Caucasian children living in the San Francisco Bay area were asked to name upper and lower case alphabet letters. The American children performed significantly better (68% vs. 50%). Both groups of children performed about the same in writing their names. A majority of them could write, completely or partially, either their family name or first name, seldom both. When tested at age 6, most of the Japanese children could read words, unless the special syllables were involved. They could say the word in one breath, sometimes after reading each character separately. When the special syllables were involved, only about a half could say the word; others could not integrate readings of two or three kana into one syllable. At the same age, the American children were administered the Metropolitan Reading Readiness Test, which does not include a test of word naming.

This means that a majority of Japanese children proceed from the half-correct character naming to the kana word naming in a year, if no special syllables are involved. This is probably because (1) the Japanese language is syllabic without stress, and (2) kana are syllabaries, and to read a word consisting of kana does not require "blending." Both points interactively enhance the development of word naming in children. It may also be advantageous that the name of each kana is the same as its reading. In CJO, to read a word by the prelexical script-sound correspondence is straightforward if the names of the characters constituting the word are known. It is necessary only to retrieve character names quickly and apply several processing rules for the special syllables (e.g., shi-ya contracts to shya). According to another survey by NLRI, children who were able to read the 46 basic kana characters could almost always read aloud a word correctly and select from four pictures the one representing the word.

However, being able to read a word consisting of kana characters does not mean that one can read and comprehend a sentence. The NLRI investigators found that, when children had just mastered the reading of the ordinary syllables represented by the 71 kana characters, they tended to read a sentence character-by-character, with short breaks. When they had mastered all the special syllables, they could read a sentence fluently by dividing it into sentence segments. Comprehension of a sentence was not easy, however. When children had mastered the basic 46 kana, they could hardly comprehend the meaning of a sentence comprised of these characters only. There were only a few exceptional children who could understand the meaning of a sentence that included some characters they could not pronounce.

There are several possible explanations for the gap between character naming and sentence comprehension. First, the speed of retrieval of the sound from each character seems critical. If the retrieval takes a long time, it will be difficult to recognize words and especially their relationship to each other, as suggested by the verbal efficiency model of reading skill (Perfetti & Lesgold, 1977). Second, the retrieval of the sound, especially when the special syllable-processing rules are to be applied, requires so much attention that higher-order syntactic and semantic processing becomes difficult. There are not enough resources left, because the child spends so much mental effort reading aloud the sentence. As Danks and Hill (1981) put it, the child is unable "to satisfy both the verbal performance and the comprehension tasks at the same time," because the performance demand is too great. This may be related to a third variable of the metacognitive goal for reading for children. At least some children do not know that reading is for meaning, that it is "a way to interpret the world" (Cole & Griffin, 1983), and they are satisfied with their being able to read aloud. Measuring variables related to those explanations and examining them, in relation to children's later reading development, appear worthwhile efforts (see Lesgold & Resnick, 1981). But, as far as I know, no such empirical studies have been conducted in Japan.

How well could the children surveyed by NLRI write? The distribution of the numbers of kana characters they could write is shown in Figure 5.6. The distribution is inverse J-shaped for children one year younger than grade K: Most children could write almost none of the characters. At grade K, some improvement occurred, but none of the 1399 children tested could write all 71 characters.

Since 1967, when the nationwide survey was conducted, the severe competition to enter prestigious universities has exerted a growing influence on early childhood education. As a result, young children's ability to read and write probably has been facilitated, directly or indirectly, by parents and educators (see Koura et al., 1978). However, this general facilitation will not change the sequence and patterns of acquisition. For example, basic kana reading is acquired first, reading special syllables is hard, reading characters is a necessary but not sufficient condition for sentence comprehension, and writing lags far behind reading.

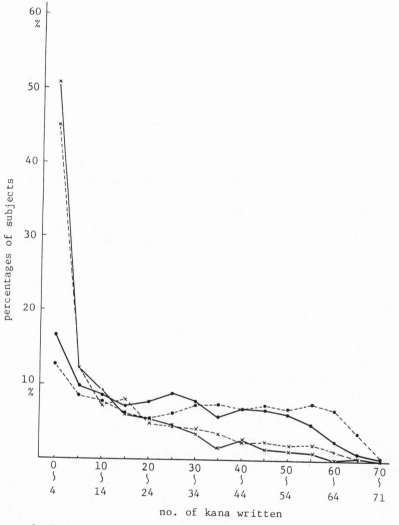

FIG. 5.6. Distribution of number of kana characters written by young children (from NLRI, 1972).

Phonetic Awareness and Learning to Read

What are the cognitive prerequisites for children to acquire literacy? The ability to discriminate characters is no doubt one of them, but it does not seem critical, because, it is assumed, children have already acquired this ability several years earlier than learning to read. Like many investigators in the field of literacy acquisition, I assume that phonetic awareness in children and/or their ability to recognize a certain phoneme or combination of phonemes, as well as ability for phonetic articulation, are necessary and usually critical prerequisites for learning to read. For CJO acquisition, the ability to syllabify and recognize a specific syllable seem essential.

Amano (1970), deriving his basic ideas from Elkonin (1956/1963), conducted two interesting experiments directly relevant to this point. In the first experiment, the ability to separate a word into syllables was investigated with 60 children from three to five years of age. The experimenter, with a lampboard containing two parallel rows of eight lamps each and two switch boxes, first showed a picture describing the referent of the target word, pronounced the word slowly, pausing between syllables, and turned on one lamp for each syllable pronounced. Then the child was required to imitate the experimenter, syllabifying the word aloud and switching on the same number of lamps in the lower row. If the child failed to do this, the procedure was repeated up to five times. All the children over four and a half years of age could, with the help of this apparatus, syllabify almost perfectly any word containing ordinary syllables only. For the three-year-olds this task of syllabication was very difficult, especially when a word contained more than three syllables.

In the second experiment, the experimenter used a picture with a row of squares below it. All words contained ordinary syllables. There were as many squares as syllables in the word represented by the picture. After short training, the child was required to syllabify a word aloud while putting small wooden blocks in the squares that corresponded to the articulated syllable. If the child performed this correctly, he or she was asked whether the syllable *ko* was involved in the word and which block corresponded to *ko*. In another task, after the child had divided a word into syllables, he or she was asked to say what the first, middle and last syllables were. If we plot the relation between children's ability to syllabify or to recognize *ko* with that of reading kana characters, we see that, irrespective of chronological age, these two abilities were closely related. Figure 5.7 illustrates that children's ability to syllabify a word improved rapidly from 60% correct when they could read almost none to the asymptote of more than 90% correct when they had learned 21–25 kana characters. Syllabic recognition was harder than syllabication: Twenty percent of the children who could not read kana at all could recognize *ko*, and fewer than 70% of the children could do so when they had

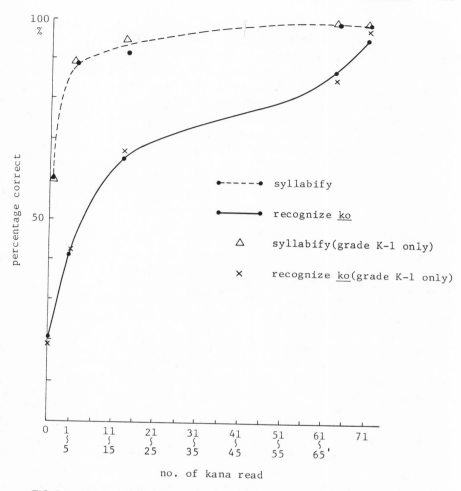

FIG. 5.7   Relationship between children's ability to syllabify or to recognize *ko* and that of reading kana characters (from Amano, 1970).

learned 21–25 kana. Identification of the first and last syllables showed similar trends but proved a little easier than recognizing *ko*.

It was concluded that children can analyze the syllabic structure of words to some extent, even when they cannot read kana at all, but no children unable to syllabify can read kana. This suggests that the act of analyzing the syllabic structure of words is "one of the most important components of the ability to learn Japanese syllabic characters" (Amano, 1970). Though this conclusion sounds tenable, it must be examined empirically. We need a longitudinal study, with later kana reading as the criterion, in which one's prior abilities to syllabify and to recognize a specific syllable are predictors and are compared with other candidate predictors. We also need a study to test whether training in these abilities will actually enhance kana reading acquisition. Regrettably, these studies have yet to be conducted, except for Amano's (1969, 1977) pilot training experiments for ordinary syllables and long syllables (Amano, 1978), all of which obtained promising results. In his first experiment, for example, a small number of 4-year-olds who were able to read virtually no kana were given short-term instruction in kana reading, with or without prior training in syllabication and syllabic recognition. The prior training had facilitative effects for those less advanced in syllabic awareness. In fact, unless children were able to recognize the first syllable of a given word, the instruction did not work.

Ecology of Literacy Acquisition

Though formal instruction for reading hiragana characters starts at grade 1, many children have acquired the ability to read most of the characters informally by that time, as the NLRI surveys demonstrate. Where does this informal acquisition take place? What activities and materials facilitate the acquisition?

According to a questionnaire survey by the NLRI (1972), fewer than 20% of all the surveyed parents reported that they actively taught their children to read characters, and they often did so by using a workbook. Most of the parents only gave their children picture books, bought kana blocks, read books to them, and answered children's questions about the characters. Direct teaching was not more effective than arranging the environment by providing books, blocks, or both, but for boys either was slightly more facilitative than doing nothing (although there was no effect for girls). Similarly, reading is directly taught in less than 20% of the kindergartens, but written hiragana can often be seen there, and children's questions about the characters are welcomed by almost all teachers.

The Hess-Azuma study (Azuma et al., 1981) enables us to compare the literacy acquisition environment at home in the United States and in Japan. From the interview with mothers conducted when the target children were 3.8 years of age, the environment seemed more favorable for literacy acquisition in the U.S. than in Japan. For example, U.S. mothers subscribed to magazines and read books to their children much more often than their Japanese counterparts. The language environment index derived from these behaviors revealed a significant difference favoring the U.S. It was positively correlated with the child's reading ability at 5.0 years and 6.0 years in both countries, suggesting its validity.

High availability of kana characters in young children's daily life seems important, at least in terms of interest in the characters. Prior to this exposure to kana, Japanese children may have learned through exposure to kanji that characters have meanings, because in our society such things as eye-catching name plates and train station sign boards are written in kanji. However, this metacognition tends to be rather global understanding, because kanji not only are figuratively complex but also appear in limited, often single contexts. On the other hand, kana characters can be familiar and recognizable through repeated appearances in varied contexts.

Sumio (1983) presents several observations of children's initial interest in characters. Each child was interested in a printed word, often his or her name or a distinctive expression in a highly familiar story. The child learned the name of a specific character in the word and recognized that character in other contexts. Whether the visual recognition of a specific character leads to learning to read depends on the child's phonetic awareness. If, and only if, the child can extract the first syllable from a familiar word, can the association between the name-pronunciation of a character (e.g., く is pronounced *ku*) and the word starting with it (*kuri* or く'), chestnut) on a kana block or kana card be meaningful. Moreover, if the child can retrieve the name of the object described on a block or card, or a familiar expression in a picture book, then he or she can infer the name-pronunciation of the character accompanying it, or meaningfully incorporate an adult's answer to questions about the character. This kind of meaningful, self-organized learning seems to play an important part in the acquisition of CJO. As Resnick (1979) put it, children are "inventing" or discovering reading processes.

Kana blocks are also useful in later stages of acquisition. After learning the names-pronunciations of several kana characters, a child can construct new combinations of them very easily. It is often great fun to find out that some combinations, which are transformed into sequence of sounds utilizing the learned script-sound correspondence, are meaningful words and others are nonsense syllables. This may lead the child to realize that any word can be represented by a combination of kana characters. The perceived utility, based on the specific knowledge about already learned characters, will certainly motivate the child to learn further.

Unlike a phoneme, a syllable is easily understood. Several forms of verbal play that enhance understanding of syllables are also available in children's daily life. One of them is *shiritori* (cap verses), in which one has to say a word beginning with the last syllable of the immediately preceding word. This provides practice in extracting the first and last syllable of words. Muto and Fujiwara (in preparation) found that: (1) when individually tested, three-year-olds could seldom produce proper responses; however, (2) in group play of *shiritori,* improper responses were often corrected by older peers, and this often led younger ones to give the proper word. *Sakasauta* (reverse singing) is another form of verbal play where the order of syllables is reversed within melodic segments. It probably enhances children's phonetic articulation.

In contrast, there is almost no rhyming activity in the Japanese language, either playfully or seriously. To make a poem in Japanese the usual way is to manipulate the number of syllables (or morae) in segments. Five and seven syllables (or morae) are basic rhythmic units. The shortest form of Japanese poem is 5–7–5 syllables and is called *haiku*. So, Japanese poetic activities are relevant not to the extraction of a phonetic element, but to syllabication. As Bradley and Bryant (1983) claim, verbal play that enhances children's phonetic awareness creates readiness for learning to read, but critical content of the play activities may vary from language to language and from orthography to orthography.

FROM CJO TO SJO

As described in the preceding section, Japanese children can, because of the nature of CJO, learn to read fairly easily. However, there is still another orthography for them to learn. In order to read ordinary books, magazines, and newspapers and to write in a mature fashion, one has to be an expert in the Standard Japanese Orthography (SJO). The acquisition of the latter takes many years.

SJO involves a great number of kanji. Therefore, expertise in SJO includes learning to read and write these complex-shaped characters. In addition, because kanji are morphograms, one has to learn their prototypal meanings. This is what knowing kanji in Japanese primarily means. In a sense, children learn the Japanese "formal conceptual structure" through kanji. The morphograms constitute a complex network of concepts, ideas, and beliefs — in short, a condensed set of cognitive tools of the culture. Moreover, choosing the right kanji among many characters sharing the same pronunciation while writing and, to a lesser extent, choosing the right pronunciation while reading are possible only with this knowledge of their prototypal meanings.

Furthermore, as our experiments described earlier suggest, expertise in SJO includes: (1) the acquisition of the compounding schemata by which kanji are combined to make new words with more extended and/or precise meanings; and (2) the cognitive skills to use both prototypal meanings of component kanji and also the schemata to solve homonymic ambiguity and to infer the meaning of unfamiliar words, sometimes by assigning likely kanji to a word in the phonetic code.

These skills apparently require a lot of practice and, in fact, much time is devoted to SJO acquisition in Japanese elementary school. However, it is doubtful whether each of these significant aspects of expertise is assigned a proper amount of instructional time. It is also disputable whether they are, or should be, explicitly taught in the classroom. Let me describe some of the ways in which children seem to acquire expertise in SJO.

First, to associate a kanji with one of its readings is fairly easy. If children spend time reading books, they are likely to learn the readings of many kanji outside the formal instruction at school. Thus, some children are much more advanced than their agemates and the academic standard. One subject in the intensive NLRI (1972) study, a six-year-old boy, could read 566 kanji in addition to hiragana, katakana, Arabic numerals and English alphabet letters. It was reported that he could read an adults' newspaper without much difficulty; he also read correspondence from his kindergarten teacher to his parents, as well as plans for the day's or week's activities posted at the entrance of the school office. He said that he had learned these kanji by reading books in which hiragana were attached to kanji, because he liked books so much. His parents' educational principle was laissez-faire. They had recognized his first interest in characters when he was a little more than a year old and helped him read a letter at 2 years. They had always responded to his questions about characters but did not intervene in his learning. Takagi (1983) also found that most second graders knew quite a few kanji that were to be introduced in third grade or later.

Second, even though the prototypal meaning of a kanji is not explicitly taught but left to be discovered by children, some of them can quickly catch it through induction or semantic analogy. For example, the little boy described earlier understood that the prototypal meaning of 停 is stoppage, when he learned that the meaning of 停電 is electricity stoppage. He said, with a smile, "(this must be) the same as 停 in 停車 (i.e., the stopping of a car)."

Compound schemata are not explicitly taught either, but, again, it is not hard for some children to acquire them by induction or analogy. It is easy for a child to infer analogically that x 肉 (x-meat) means "meat of x," using a primitive, concept-specific compounding schema, when he or she has learned that 牛肉 (cow-meat) means "beef" and 豚肉 (pig-meat) means "pork." As a child accumulates learning experiences about kanji compound words, compounding schemata become more and more abstract and generally applicable.

Finally, using kanji in inferring the meaning of an unfamiliar word given aurally or in resolving homonymic ambiguity when the target has homonyms may seem difficult, but in fact it is not. For kanji compound words, there is a big gap between ease of reading and of writing, even when a very lenient criterion is applied to the latter (e.g., accepting a character that is recognizable but which has some incorrect details). This probably implies that in some entries of the mental lexicon the kanji code is not described in its complete form but has to be assembled at the time of writing. For this assembling, the critical step is the selection of the appropriate kanji out of the many kanji with the same sounds. Data by Yoshida, Matsuda and Shimura (1975) showed that most dictation errors involved choosing identically pronounced but different characters and that those who could retrieve many characters satisfying a given phonetic code tended to perform well in dictation. This skill in choosing for a known word a semantically appropriate character that satisfies the phonetic constraint can be extended to skills necessary for inferring the meaning of aurally given unfamiliar words and for differentiating a word from its homonyms by assigning proper kanji. Our data (Kojima & Hatano, in preparation-b) demonstrate that seventh graders could infer reasonably well the meaning of unfamiliar words given in kana, probably by assigning appropriate kanji, and their performance differed only slightly from that of college students. However, because these aspects of SJO expertise are not given sufficient time in the classroom and are often not taught explicitly, there are large individual differences in the extent of mastery (See Japan Teachers' Union, 1976; Stevenson, Stigler, Lucker, & Lee, 1983).

I claim that Makita's (1968) often-cited assertion that there are only a negligible number of children with reading disability in Japan must be doubted. In fact, he did not give any test of reading comprehension to children. CJO may be easier than English orthography for beginners, but having to learn SJO in addition to CJO, without intensive, explicit teaching may be a burden for a substantial member of Japanese children.

As suggested from the foregoing discussion, the most difficult aspect of SJO acquisition is learning to write kanji accurately. In addition, because being able to write kanji properly is regarded by our culture as a sign of cognitive maturity and general understanding, school teachers tend to spend an undue amount of time practicing the writing of kanji. Kanji dictation quizzes are given very often, sometimes every day. A student is punished for making an error by having to write the kanji many times. Kanji are acquired by repeated writing. In fact, as revealed by *kusho* behavior (i.e., writing in kanji in the air), figural memory of kanji is enhanced by this motor element (Sasaki & Watanabe, 1983). Practice in writing kanji is usually mechanical and boring. Most shcool children do not really understand why they have to learn to write so many kanji, except for preparing for exams or obtaining cultural respect.

It is sometimes argued that a Japanese-language word processor, now being accepted in the business world, will have profound effects on SJO and instruction in its expertise. To use the contemporary version of the word processor, one has to input every word or sentence segment in kana. To get kanji transcription, one inputs the corresponding kana and hits the conversion key. When only one corresponding kanji transcription is registered, it appears automatically. When there are two or more alternatives, as is often the case, they are shown in the order of frequency or by some other measure of likelihood. One can choose the right kanji by hitting the selection key. Thus, unlike conventional handwriting, kanji transcription by a word processor is always mediated by the phonetic code. Moreover, the reader can ignore figural details of the character, because he or she is required to choose only the right one. As mentioned, memory of kanji has a motor element, and the disuse of this element may make the memory, especially its visual imagery aspect, less stable. These features of word processing may make the user incompetent to write kanji by hand. This strongly suggests that the word processor should not be introduced into the classroom. However, with it we may be able to save a great amount of the time now being spent in learning to write kanji.

CONCLUSIONS

The following three conclusions can be derived from the above discussion. Though the present chapter has mostly concerned the Japanese language, any of the conclusions, in principle, may be generalized across cultures and languages.

1. The standard Japanese orthography is, in the fundamental sense, rational, though it may seem irrational and unnecessarily complicated. The use of kanji in addition to kana is well justified. I must assume any orthography that has survived for hundreds of years must be rational. This rationality provides a basis for self-organized acquisition of literacy. The standard Japanese orthography, which is contrained by the language, favors experienced readers over beginners or writers. An orthography unavoidably gives priority to some goals over others, since there are multiple, often incompatible, goals for it to fulfill. There is no single "optimal" orthography. That the Japanese orthography is rational does not mean it is (almost) optimal—judgment of optimality must depend on the criterial goals.

2. The processes through which one comes to be able to read and write fluently utilizing orthographic knowledge are cognitively universal but culturally and linguistically specialized. For example, learning to read universally presupposes (or at least is greatly facilitated by) the child's phonetic awareness and/or classifying and recognizing some phonetic aspects of the language. At the same time, which aspects are critical vary from language to language. A syllabic language like Japanese does not require phonemic classification or recognition but does need syllabication and syllabic identification for literacy acquisition. Moreover, what kinds of play activities and materials are facilitative also vary culturally as well as linguistically.

3. The (Japanese) orthography is an integral part of the (Japanese) culture, and the acquisition of the orthography is thus enhanced in various ways by various cultural elements. School instruction constitutes only one, sometimes minor, cultural element.

ACKNOWLEDGMENTS

An earlier version of this paper was presented at the Houston conference on Learning to Read: Cognitive Universals and Cultural Constraints, April 1984. The author would like to thank Professor Barbara Foorman and other participants of the conference and also Professors Kayoko Inagaki and Keiko Kojima for their helpful comments.

REFERENCES

Amano, K. (1969). [*Instruction and the formation of learning ability: The case of learning to read kana characters.*] Paper presented at the 33rd Annual Convention of Japanese Psychological Association, Tokyo, Japan.

Amano, K. (1970). [Formation of the act of analyzing phonemic structures of words and its relation to learning Japanese syllabic characters (KANAMOJI).] *Japanese Journal of Educational Psychology, 18,* 76–89.

Amano, K. (1977). [On the formation of the act of analyzing the syllabic structure of words and the learning of Japanese syllabic characters in moderately mentally retarded children.] *Japanese Journal of Educational Psychology, 25,* 73–84.

Amano, K. (1978). [*On the formation of the act of analyzing the syllabic structure of words and the learning of Japanese syllabic characters — Acquisition of the "awareness" of long syllables and learning to read words involving those syllables.*] Paper presented at the 20th Annual Convention of Japanese Association of Educational Psychology, Yokohama, Japan.

Azuma, H., Kashiwagi, K., & Hess, R. D. (1981). [*Relations between maternal attitudes and behaviors and child's cognitive development.*] Tokyo: University of Tokyo Press.

Baddeley, A. D., & Lieberman, K. (1980). Spatial working memory. In Nickerson, R. S. (Ed.), *Attention and performance VIII.* (pp. 521–539). Hillsdale, NJ.: Lawrence Erlbaum Associates.

Bradley, L. & Bryant, P. E. (1983). Categorizing sounds and learning to read — a causal connection. *Nature, 301*(5899), 419–421.

Brooks, L. R. (1967). The suppression of visualization by reading. *Quarterly Journal of Experimental Psychology, 19,* 289–299.

Cole, M., & Griffin, P. (1983). A socio-historical approach to remediation. *The Quarterly Newsletter of the Laboratory of Comparative Human Cognition, 5,* 69–74.

Danks, J. H., & Hill G. O. (1981). Interactive models of lexical access during oral reading. In A. M. Lesgold & C. A. Perfetti (Eds.), *Interactive processes in reading.* (pp. 131–154). Hillsdale, NJ: Lawrence Erlbaum Associates.

Elkonin, D. B. (1956/1963). The psychology of mastering the elements of reading. In B. Simon & J. Simon (Eds.), *Educational psychology in the USSR.* (pp. 165–179). London: Routledge & Kegan Paul.

Glushko, R. J. (1979). Cognitive and pedagogical implications of orthography. *The Quarterly Newsletter of the Laboratory of Comparative Human Cognition, 1,*(2), 22–26.

Hatano, G., Kuhara, K., & Akiyama, M. (1981). *Kanji* help readers of Japanese infer the meaning of unfamiliar words. *The Quarterly Newsletter of the Laboratory of Comparative Human Cognition, 3*(2), 30–33.

Imura, T. (1943). Aphasia: Characteristic symptoms in Japan. *Journal of Psychiatric Neurology, 47,* 196–218.

Iwata, M. (1976). [Reading and writing: Neurology of character processing.] *Kagaku (Science), 46,* 405–410.

Japan Teachers' Union. (1976). [A survey report of achievement for improvement of the course of study.] *Kyoiku-hyoron (Educational Review),* extra number in July.

Kitao, N. (1960). [Comparative study on readability of "hiragana-bun" and "kanji-majiri-bun."] *Japanese Journal of Educational Psychology, 7,* 195–199.

Kleiman, G. M. (1975). Speech recoding in reading. *Journal of Verbal Learning and Verbal Behavior, 14,* 323–339.

Kojima, K., & Hatano, G. (in preparation-a). Transcription recoding in language processing: The use of kanji code in inferring the meaning of an aurally given unfamiliar word.

Kojima, K., & Hatano, G. (in preparation-b). Inferring the meaning of an unfamiliar word by tentatively assigning kanji: A developmental study.

Koura, I., Kobayashi, T., Kobayashi, Y., Tanaka, T., Sugimura, T., Muraishi, S., Matsukura, S., Noda, H. & Fujita, K. (1978). [Symposium: On the problem of letter teaching in early childhood.] *Annual Report of Educational Psychology in Japan, 17,* 79–83.

Kuhara, K., & Hatano, G. (1981). *Comprehension and memory of a short oral discourse involving homonymic ambiguity: Effects of headings.* Paper presented at the American Educational Research Association meeting in Los Angeles.

National Institute for Language Research. (1972). [*Reading and writing ability in preschool children.*] Tokyo: Tokyo Shoseki.

Lesgold, A. M., & Resnick, L. B. (1981). *How reading difficulties develop: Perspectives from a longitudinal study.* Pittsburgh: Learning Research Development Center, University of Pittsburgh.

Makita, K. (1968). The rarity of reading disability in Japanese children. *American Journal of Orthopsychiatry, 38,* 599–614.

Muraishi, S. (1971). [Acquisition of spoken and written language by young children. In. T. Fujinaga, S. Muraishi, & H. Saiga Eds., *Handbook of early education, vol 4: Language and number.*] (pp. 25–37). Tokyo: Shogakkan.

Muto, T., & Fujiwara, H. (in preparation). Cognitive and social factors in verbal play of *shiritori* (cap verses).

Perfetti, C. A., & Lesgold, A. M. (1977). Discourse comprehension and sources of individual differences. In M. A. Just & P. A. Carpenter (Eds.), *Cognitive processes in comprehension.* (pp. 141–183). Hillsdale, NJ: Lawrence Erlbaum Associates.

Resnick, L. B. (1979). Toward a usable psychology of reading instruction. In L. B. Resnick & P. A. Weaver (Eds.), *Theory and practice of early reading,* Vol. 3. (pp. 355–372). Hillsdale, NJ: Lawrence Erlbaum Associates.

Rubenstein, H., Lewis, S. S., & Rubenstein, M. A. (1971). Evidence for phonemic recoding in visual word recognition. *Journal of Verbal Learning and Verbal Behavior, 10,* 647–657.

Saito, H. (1981). [Use of graphemic and phonemic encoding in reading *Kanji* and *Kana.*] *Japanese Journal of Psychology, 52,* 266–273.

Sasaki, M., & Watanabe, A. (1983). [An experimental study of spontaneous writing-like behavior ("KUSHO") in Japanese.] *Japanese Journal of Educational Psychology, 31,* 273–282.

Sasanuma, S., & Fujimura, O. (1971). Selective impairment of phonetic and non-phonetic transcription of words in Japanese aphasic patients: *Kana* vs. *Kanji* in visual recognition and writing. *Cortex, 7,* 1–18.

Sasanuma, S., & Monoi, H. (1975). The syndrome of Gogi (word meaning) aphasia: Selective impairment of kanji processing. *Neurology, 25,* 627–632.

Stevenson, H. W., Stigler, J. M., Lucker, G. W., & Lee, S. (1981). Reading disabilities: The case of Chinese, Japanese and English. *University of Michigan/University of Chicago Cognitive Science Technical Report,* No. 31.

Sumio, K. (1983). [Picture books to stimulate early reading: Initial discovery and independent reading skills.] *The Science of Reading, 27,* 20–30.

Suzuki, T. (1975). On the twofold phonetic realization of basic concepts: In defense of Chinese characters in Japanese. In P. C. C. Peng (Ed.), *Language in Japanese society.* (pp. 175–192).

Tokyo: University of Tokyo Press.

Suzuki, T. (1977). Writing is not language, or is it? *Journal of Pragmatics, 1,* 407–420.

Suzuki, T. (1978). [Are Kanji compound words loan words from Chinese?] *Gekkan Gengo (Language Monthly), 7*(2), 2–8.

Takagi, K. (1983). [*Acquisition of knowledge through informal learning:Analysis of familiarity ratings by 2nd-graders of kanji words yet to be learned.*] Paper presented at the 25th Annual Convention of Japanese Association of Educational Psychology, Kumamoto.

Umemura, C. (1981). [Functional properties of Japanese letters (Kana and Kanji) in memory studies.] *Japanese Journal of Educational Psychology, 29,* 123–131.

Yoshida, A., Matsuda, Y., & Shimura, M. (1975). [A study on instruction of Chinese characters: An approach from an analysis of children's errata.] *School of Education Research Bulletin, University of Tokyo, 14,* 221–251.

6

Non-Alphabetic Codes in Learning to Read: The Case of the Japanese

Barbara R. Foorman
University of Houston

Why should a book on learning to read include a chapter on how Japanese children learn to read? The reason is that there are two different kinds of scripts in Japanese—the kana syllabary and the kanji logographs—which seem to impose different psychological demands on the reading process, demands that appear confounded in the English alphabetic script. The common assumption is that kanji is processed visually and kana, with its regular sound-symbol correspondences, is processed auditorily. This assumed auditory/visual split prompted Makita's (1968) claim that there were no reading disabilities in Japan and encouraged Rozin, Poritsky, and Sotsky (1971) to remediate inner-city second graders with material written as Chinese characters. For Kimura and Bryant (1983 + page 65 this volume), Japanese orthography's visual/auditory split provided a test of the importance of phonological segmentation in children's reading and also of the significance of the experimental procedure called concurrent vocalization. They reasoned that concurrent vocalization specifically disrupts phonological processing and, therefore, should impede reading and writing kana but not kanji. This is indeed what happened, and they also found that concurrent vocalization interrupted writing, but not reading, English. Hence, they concluded that prelexical phonological analysis does not appear essential for reading English.

The heuristic value of experiments contrasting Japanese and English orthography is clear: By looking at cultural differences in learning to read, we can test hypotheses about psychological processes in our models of reading. And the auditory versus visual strategies encouraged by the kana and kanji codes allow us to focus on the role of phonological segmentation in a way not allowed by the English alphabet, where auditory and visual strategies are hard to separate. But heuristic value alone does not justify an experiment. The results must be valid. Just as Makita's (1968) claim about the lack of reading disabilities in Japan has been challenged by Stevenson, Stigler, Lucker, Lee, Hsu, and Kitamura's (1982) research and just as Rozin et al.'s (1971) success with Chinese characters does not necessarily "eliminate certain general interpretations of dyslexia, for example, as a visual-auditory memory deficit" (p. 105), we must be willing to reexamine the basic assumption underlying all of this work—that kana is processed auditorially and kanji is processed visually. Professor Hatano's chapter provides us with just this sort of reexamination.

Characteristics of Japanese Orthographies

Let's review what Professor Hatano has to tell us about how Japanese children learn to read. He discusses the processes through which Japanese children come to read and write Japanese sentences fluently, using knowledge of its orthography. He points out that the syllabic code of kana and the morphographic code of kanji invoke processes not invoked by the English alphabet code. But he also points out that in spite of these orthographic differences there are many processes in common to learning to read Japanese and learning to read English. In the words of this volume's title, there are cognitive universals as well as cultural constraints in learning to read.

Professor Hatano characterizes Japanese as having two orthographies: Standard Japanese Orthography (SJO) and Children's Japanese Orthography (CJO). SJO is acquired during the elementary and secondary grades and allows replacement of kana with kanji *wherever the Japanese language allows*. The Japanese spoken language and Chinese spoken language are completely different. Between the eigth and ninth centuries A.D., Japanese emmissaries who were sent by the Imperial Court to China brought back many elements of the culture, including the writing system. During the next century, Japanese scholars developed a syllabary system, composed of modified characters, to represent the sounds of the Japanese language. These modified characters are called hiragana. They help integrate Chinese characters into the Japanese language. In the nineteenth century another syllabary was invented so that foreign words could be represented within the Japanese sound system. This recent syllabary is called katakana. For example, the English word "coffee" is written in Katakana as コーヒー and is pronounced "kohee."

A typical Japanese sentence, therefore, almost always incorporates kanji and hiragana and often katakana. The sentence, "We drink coffee," is written in SJO by using the katakana code for "coffee," followed by the hiragana symbol representing the objective case particle (i.e., を, "(w)o"), followed by the word "drink," where the root of the word is represented by a kanji (飲)

and the present tense inflection is represented by three hiragana symbols (ﾞﾗｰ). We can write the kanji for the word "to drink" in hiragana and thus express the sentence in Children's Japanese Orthography (CJO).

Instruction in Japanese Orthographies

The kanji for "nomu," to drink, is introduced in third or fourth grade with the hiragana symbols alongside it as an aid to pronunciation and meaning. Most children are able to recognize this kanji much earlier because of its frequent use in the language and the context clue of "coffee" in the sentence. What do you do with coffee? You drink it, of course.

Why is this kanji introduced relatively late when its usage is so common? — because, with 12 strokes, it's difficult to write. The 2,000 essential kanji introduced in elementary and secondary school are introduced instructionally, usually according to the number of strokes, going from the characters with a single stroke up to those with 23 strokes. Virtually the only exception to this pattern is the fourteenth character, which has 18 strokes. It is introduced early because it is an essential component to the kanji compounds representing the days of the week.

Complexity of a kanji is defined instructionally to a great extent by the number of its figural elements. The configuration of these elements is practically burned into the neurology of Japanese school children by constant drill and practice. In addition to the number of strokes, the student is taught to pay attention to the order in which the strokes are made and the overall spatial plan of the character. Beyond these components of necessary penmanship are the aesthetics of beautiful writing — calligraphy. Japanese today will tell you that calligraphy is a dying art form. But in the last four years I have been in classrooms in Hokkaido, Honshu, and Kyushu, where calligraphy was an integral part of the curriculum (Foorman & Kinoshita, 1983; Foorman, 1983). And beyond the required curriculum, there are calligraphy clubs and local, regional, and national calligraphy contests.

In addition to learning the visuo-spatial representation of kanji, the child is also taught the *on* (Sino-Japanese) and *kun* (Japanese) reading for the character. For example, the *on* reading for the verb "to drink" is *in*, while the *kun* reading is *nomu*. As Professor Hatano points out, the Japanese reading is referred to as the semantic reading, whereas the Chinese reading is often called the phonetic reading. Also, as Professor Hatano points out, many kanji have the same *on* (Chinese) reading. As he said, 70 of the 2,000 essential kanji have the Chinese reading *ko*. In spoken Chinese, the number of the homonyms is reduced through the language's use of pitch; in spoken Japanese, potential ambiguity is alleviated by the context-determined use of the Japanese reading. The important point here is that no potential ambiguity exists in written Japanese. Each kanji has its unique meeeting.

To some extent, we can see a parallel in English. There are words whose meanings we understand when we see them in print but whose pronunciation eludes us because we have never had to say them aloud. Our inability to pronounce the word might get us into trouble when it comes time to spell it. As Kimura and Bryant's (1983, p. 152) research suggests: ". . . English children may read single words without the help of prelexical phonological construction, much as Japanese children must read kanji without the help of phonological analysis; and [their work suggests] that English children may write words on the basis of letter-sound correspondences," similar to the way Japanese children write kana. Thus, phonological segmentation, long thought to be a crucial element in learning to read (Bradley & Bryant, 1978, 1983; Goldstein, 1976; Liberman, Shankweiler, Fisher, & Carter, 1974; Lundberg, Olofsson, & Wall, 1980) may not be so crucial. As Barron and Baron (1977) claimed and, as the Kimura and Bryant (1983) study suggests, phonological segmentation may be more relevant to writing. Thus, as Perfetti (1985 and Chapter 1, this volume) suggests, lexical access may indeed be the centrally recurring aspect of reading in English as well as Japanese.

Processing Japanese Orthographies

According to Professor Hatano, for the experienced reader, there are four internal codes of a word: (1) the kanji code, (2) the kana code, (3) the phonetic code, and (4) the meaning code. The kana code and the phonetic code are directly interchangeable, but there are times when the kanji code might intervene. Let's consider how kana processing might access meaning directly through the kanji code. Kana's 71 syllables provide one-to-one sound-symbol correspondence and, hence, fairly easy access to meaning through the phonetic code. But, as Professor Hatano explains, the correspondence is not perfect, because some kana are blended to form special syllables and exceptions in pronunciation exist for three kana representing case particles.

Yet the task of learning to pronounce kana is not a difficult one. Comprehending them, however, is more difficult, Hatano reasons, because attentional demands of retrieving sounds from each character, especially the special ones, is great. Also, the practice in CJO instruction of reading kana outloud interferes with a central metacognitive goal of reading — that reading is for meaning.

We now see that pronouncing and comprehending kana are not so easy as generally presumed. But what about the possibility that kana can be accessed through the kanji code? Hatano presents this possibility as he discusses the latent cognitive function of kanji. He explains that readers can understand unfamiliar words spoken or written in kana because of kanji codes stored in long-term memory. The use of these stores is particularly convenient in cases of homonymic ambiguity. The reader or listener accesses all relevant representations of kanji that fit the target pronunciation and selects the one whose meaning best fits the context. Many times I have seen Japanese draw kanji in the air or in their hands so that the persons with whom they are speaking can verify their choice — the so-called "kusho" behavior. But, as Hatano points out, such latent cognitive functions of kanji require acquisition of at least the 2,000 essential kanji, mental storage space for these kanji, and strategies to apply this stored information. Clearly, a certain amount of SJO expertise and memory capacity is required if kana are to be accessed through the kanji code. Of course, in cases where homonymic ambiguity does not exist, kana would more likely be processed immediately through the phonetic code. But the fact that blind college students who had never learned to read or write kanji were spontaneously able to refer to kanji (as were preschool children who had not been taught kanji) strongly underlines the crucial role of kanji in Japanese life.

Apparently one cannot simply say that kana are processed by the phonetic code. Is it equally simplistic to say that kanji are processed directly by the meaning code? First, bear in mind that by "meaning code" Professor Hatano means a formal conceptual structure. And he believes that "children learn the Japanese 'formal conceptual structure' through kanji, because morphograms constitute a complex network of concepts, ideas, and beliefs — in short, a condensed set of cognitive tools of the culture" (p. 108 this volume). The question to be raised is, to what extent is this meaning code cognitively universal or linguistically constrained by the Japanese language? Perhaps the answer is that kanji allow access to conceptual universals through their prototypal meanings, that is, through their Japanese readings.

The Issue of Phonological Awareness

Let me underscore the significance of Professor Hatano's chapter. For the first time in English we have an in-depth discussion of the cognitive processing demands of reading kana and kanji for novices and experts in the Japanese culture. In the 1960s, discussions of the Japanese orthographies focused on the belief that alphabets were optimally efficient, and writing systems had evolved from logographies to syllabaries to alphabets (Gelb, 1963; see Gibson & Levin, 1975; Henderson, 1982; Taylor, 1981). Such a viewpoint leads to the claim that the Japanese orthographies are fixated at the syllabary stage because "this sequence of the stages of writing reflects the stages of primitive psychology . . . the division of syllables into single sounds usually lies beyond their capacity" (Gelb, 1963, p. 203). In the 1970s, the discussion of orthographic efficiency swung 180 degrees in the opposite direction, with psychologists such as Gleitman and Rozin (1973, 1977) teaching children to read with an invented English syllabary utilizing pictographs and logographs. They attribute the children's success with the rebus system to the regularity of sound-symbol correspondence and the more direct access to meaning. Yet, we are left wondering to what extent processing was facilitated by ease of phonological segmentation or by distinctiveness of visual form or by the so-called Hawthorne Effect of being taught a new system.

In the 1980s, we are benefitting from a sophisticated investigation of the interaction between orthographic processing and cultural factors. The development of valid and reliable cross-cultural tests allows us, for the first time to compare reading achievement in Japan and the United States (See Lee, Stigler, & Stevenson, Ch. 7, this volume). Professor Hatano's discussion of kana and kanji within the context of an information processing model of reading and within the eco-cultural demands of Japanese culture and schooling help us to interpret the Japanese children's higher mean achievement on their tests. The Japanese first and fifth graders in the study were moving from Children's Japanese Orthography (CJO) to Standard Japanese Orthography (SJO). In first grade, the tests were composed primarily of kana, whereas in fifth grade the number of kanji were substantial (with 700 or so of the essential kanji having been taught in school). Professor Hatano's discussion of CJO acquisition has enabled us to understand the role of phonological segmentation in learning kana and the demands imposed by the special syllables. His observation that Japanese preschoolers can analyze the phonemic structure of words to some extent before they read kana but that they cannot read kana before they are able to analyze the phonemic structure of words illustrates the importance of early segmentation ability. An unanswered question is to what extent this phonological awareness causes later kana reading and the ability to recognize specific syllables. Another unanswered question, as Professor Hatano points out, is what the precursors of phonological awareness might be in the Japanese culture. He does not believe, as Professor Bryant does, that rhyme and alliteration play a role because in the Japanese language rhyme is a concept relating to number of syllables, not intra-syllabic relationships. But Japanese children do engage in word play that seems to enhance phonological awareness.

The higher reading achievement of Japanese fifth graders (and Chinese fifth graders) in Lee et al.'s study might at first be explained on the basis of the direct access to meaning provided by kanji or additionally explained by social factors such as the culture's valuing of literacy and schooling. But Hatano's experiments on SJO expertise help us to see that the road to expertise for these fifth graders involves more than memorizing morphograms and accessing meaning directly through their (kanji) latent cognitive function. And the road to SJO expertise means more than subscribing to the culture's valuing of literacy and schooling per se. For Professor Hatano, the road to expertise involves the instantiation of kanji with their prototypal Japanese reading as the essence of Japanese culture— an essential element in a Japanese reader's identity as a member of the culture. Given the importance, then, of kanji as a "cognitive tool for the Japanese culture," it is not difficult to understand the apprehension with which Professor Hatano views the advent of word processing for Japanese. Kanji instruction emphasizes writing a character over and over until the configuration is imprinted in memory. By inputting words via kana or roman letters and hitting the kanji conversion key (see Becker, 1984), word processing alleviates the need to store figurative aspects of kanji in memory. But, without the figural representation, kanji's latent cognitive function would clearly be reduced and expertise in SJO would decline. Such a prospect is indeed daunting for a nation committed to the computer age.

REFERENCES

Barron, R., & Baron, J. (1977). How children get meaning from printed words. *Child Development, 48,* 587–594.

Becker, J. D. (1984). Multilingual word processing. *Scientific American, 251*(1), 96–107.

Bradley, L., & Bryant, P. E. (1978). Difficulties in auditory organization as a possible cause of reading backwardness. *Nature, 271,* 746–747.

Bradley, L., & Bryant, P. E. (1983). Categorizing sounds and learning to read—a causal connection. *Nature, 301,* 419–421.

Foorman, B. R. (1983). English-, Spanish-, and Japanese-speaking children's performance on perceptual and communication tasks. *Communication & Cognition, 16*(4), 381–401.

Foorman, B. R., & Kinoshita, Y. (1983). Linguistic effects on children's encoding and decoding performance in Japan, the United States, and England. *Child Development, 54,* 69–77.

Gelb, I. J. (1963). *A study of writing* (2nd ed.). Chicago: University of Chicago Press.

Gibson, E. J. & Levin, H. (1975). *The psychology of reading.* Cambridge, MA: M.I.T. Pres.

Gleitman, L. R., & Rozin, P. (1973). Teaching reading by use of a syllabary. *Reading Research Quarterly, 8,* 447–483.

Gleitman, L. R., & Rozin, P. (1977). The structure and acquisition of reading I: Relations between orthographies and the structure of language. In A. S. Reber and D. L. Scarborough (Eds.), *Toward a Psychology of Reading.* Hillsdale, NJ: Lawrence Erlbaum.

Goldstein, D. M. (1976). Cognitive-linguistic functioning and learning to read in preschools. *Journal of Educational Psychology, 68,* 680–688.

Henderson, L. (1982). *Orthography and word recognition in reading.* NY: Academic Press.

Kimura, Y., & Bryant, P. E. (1983). Reading and writing in English and Japanese: A cross-cultural study of young children. *British Journal of Developmental Psychology, 1,* 143–154.

Liberman, I. Y., Shankweiler, D., Fischer, F. W., & Carter, B. (1974). Explicit syllable and phoneme segmentation in the young child. *Journal of Experimental Child Psychology, 18,* 201–212.

Lundberg, I., Olofsson, A., & Wall, S. (1980). Reading and spelling skills in the first school years predicted from phonemic awareness skills in kindergarten. *Scandinavian Journal of Psychology, 21,* 159–173.

Makita, K. (1968). The rarity of reading disability in Japanese children. *American Journal of Orthopsychiatry, 38,* 599–614.

Perfetti, C. A. (1985). *Reading ability.* NY: Oxford University Press.

Rozin, P., Poritsky, S., & Sotsky, R. (1971). American children with reading problems can easily learn to read English represented by Chinese characters. *Science, 171,* 1264–1267.

Stevenson, H. W., Stigler, J. W., Lucker, G. W., Lee, S., Hsu, C., & Kitamura, S. (1982). Reading disabilities: The case of Chinese, Japanese and English. *Child Development, 53,* 1164–1181.

Taylor, I. (1981). Writing systems and reading. In T. G. Waller and G. E. Mackinnon (Eds.), *Reading Research: Advances in Theory and Practice.* NY: Academic Press.

7 Beginning Reading in Chinese and English

Shin-ying Lee
University of Michigan

James W. Stigler
University of Chicago

Harold W. Stevenson
University of Michigan

The purpose of this paper is to explore some of the factors involved in children's learning to read Chinese. We became involved in this area of research because of our interest in theoretical analyses of the reading process that emphasized the role of orthography in reading. Several arguments have been advanced to support a basic distinction between the processes involved in reading a logographic writing system, such as Chinese, and an alphabetic writing system, such as English. We begin with a brief discussion of these arguments.

It has been suggested that the Chinese writing system makes possible the holistic recognition of single word units. Such recognition may be difficult in English, where analytical processes are assumed to be required for decoding English words (Rozin & Gleitman, 1977). In addition, it has been argued that the logography of Chinese provides consistencies between symbol and sound, whereas the rules governing grapheme-phoneme correspondence in English orthography are complex, irregular, and difficult for beginning readers to master. As a result, reading English presents a host of problems related to phonemic awareness and segmentation and phonetic decoding. Furthermore, alphabetic languages have been considered by writers such as Gleitman and Rozin (1977) to be more complex than logographic writing systems. These writers suggest that an alphabetic writing system, such as is employed in English, uses only a small number of abstract elements, phonemes, to represent the language. Therefore, the relation of sign to meaning has to be mediated through the sound system. Phonetic decoding thereby becomes an obligatory stage in the acquisition of reading skills in English. Conversely, in a logographic writing system such as Chinese, the word itself is considered to be a distinctive unit visually, phonologically and semantically. The total perception of the symbol maps directly on to its meaning in Chinese — something that is generally prohibited in reading the sets of letters encountered in English words (Rozin, Poritsky, & Sotsky, 1971; Hatano, Kuhara, & Akiyama, 1981). Aided by the strong perceptual cues, the beginning reader of Chinese should be less dependent on phonetic decoding than the beginning reader of English.

According to this line of reasoning, learning to read Chinese characters should depend strongly on memory, while learning to read English should depend upon the child's understanding of the relation of symbol to sound — a discovery difficult for some children. The basis of this difficulty has been hypothesized to lie in two general areas: First, a certain level of phonemic awareness is required in order to grasp the concept that speech can be segmented into phonemes and that these phonemes can be represented by symbols; second, the system of rules that relates English to speech is difficult for the child to learn because it is both complex and irregular. Thus, while writing systems employing an alphabet are more efficient for fluent adults, it is proposed that they make greater conceptual demands on those beginning to read the language.

Disagreements with these proposals related to learning to read Chinese and English can be readily summoned, for many of them are based upon an overly simplistic notion of the Chinese writing system. A brief description of written Chinese is helpful in pointing out these misconceptions.

THE CHINESE WRITING SYSTEM

Chinese Logographs

We should begin by discussing the distinctions between pictographs, ideographs, and logographs. In the evolution of writing systems, pictographs are the most primitive. Only modest modifications of drawings of objects occur in pictographs. The pictograph for "person" may consist of a line representing the body and two attached lines representing legs. Combinations of pictographs may be used to express ideas. These more abstract representations are called ideographs. For example, the pictograph for roof placed over that for woman is used to represent the idea of "feeling at ease."

Written Chinese is often mistakenly referred to as an ideographic language. After thousands of years of modification and development, the Chinese writing system retains few examples of pictorial representations of concrete objects or actions. According to one authoritative estimate (Martin, 1972), only 5% of all Chinese words are represented by simple pictographs or ideographs, 5% are compound ideographs, and 90% are phonetic compounds. The Chinese writing system can be best described, not as a pictographic or an ideographic writing system, but as a logographic system, one in which characters represent the minimal meaningful units of the language (morphemes).

Words and Logographs

A second common mistaken notion is to think that a word in Chinese is represented by a single character. Writers such as Rozin and Gleitman (1977) are incorrect when they suggest that readers of English "learn to read far more words than do the Chinese" (p. 66). They base their conclusion on the fact that, whereas an average American high school student knows about 50,000 words, a literate Chinese adult knows 4,000 characters. A character is not typically equivalent to a word, for most words in modern Chinese are represented by more than a single character. Knowing 4,000 characters, therefore, makes it possible to learn many thousands of words that can be derived from combinations of the characters.

The impression is given in many Western descriptions of Chinese that the child's tasks in learning to read are to discriminate the pattern of lines that constitute a character and then to memorize the meaning attached to this pattern. But a Chinese character does not have a unitary, fixed meaning. The same character can have different meanings in different words. Let us use the character 信 as an example. When this character is written alone, one of its meanings is "letter." When it is combined with 用, which means "use," the pair means "credit." When it is combined with 心 (heart) the word represented is "faith." It is difficult to find any basis for this meaning, except for the fact that the character 信 can also mean "belief." When combined with 任, the two mean "trust," when combined with 息, the pair means "information," and, when paired with 號, the combination means "signal." Obviously, knowing one of the meanings of a Chinese character does not necessarily give the reader any assurance that it will be easy to discern the meaning of words of which any particular character is a part.

Chinese is typically written, one character after another, in vertical strings. It is not obvious to the beginning reader of Chinese which successive characters in a sequence of characters go together to form the words of a sentence. Although boundaries between words are defined in English text by one space, no cues exist in Chinese text as to which characters should be grouped into meaningful word units. Segmentation clearly is a problem for the novice in trying to decode written Chinese sentences. In English, segmentation is of phonemes within a word; in Chinese, it is segmentation of strings of characters into words. The problem of segmentation of Chinese text is apparent in Fig. 7.1, where a short story for fifth-graders is presented in both Chinese and English versions. Although sentences are separated by commas, no other cues are given about when one word ends and another begins.

有一隻驢子跟著主人進城採購，主人買了兩包棉花要牠載回家，在涉水渡河的時候，驢子想起上次主人帶牠進城買鹽時，就在回程經過這條河時，牠不小心跌了一跤，爬起來後發現背上的重量減輕了許多，原來鹽浸了水就被溶解了，所以這一次牠又想如法泡製，於是就故意跌了一跤，把整個身子泡在水裏，可是這回當牠從河裏爬起來以後，發覺背上的東西不但沒有減輕，反而加重了，原來這回棉花在水裏吸足了水分，重量便增加了好幾倍，最後驢子只得載著又濕又重的水棉花，一路上滑倒好幾次，吃足了苦頭才回到家。

Paragraph Reading and Comprehension
(Item from Fifth Grade Level)

ENGLISH

Once there was a donkey who accompanied his master to town to purchase some supplies. The master bought two sacks of cotton, which he loaded on the donkey, and they started home. After a while, they approached a stream, and the donkey suddenly recalled the accident he had experienced on a previous trip to town. On that occasion, the master had bought two heavy sacks of salt, and as they were crossing this stream, the donkey carelessly slipped and fell into the water. When he scrambled back up, he was delighted to discover that his load had become much lighter. The salt had dissolved in the water.

Hoping to achieve the same results on this trip, the donkey fell into the water deliberately, making sure he soaked his pack completely. When he came out, however, he found that his load had grown much heavier, not lighter. Instead of being washed away like the salt, the cotton absorbed the water. Now the donkey had to carry the wet, heavy cotton all the way home, and he stumbled many times before he finally made it back. In trying to save himself work, the donkey had only managed to make things worse.

Paragraph Reading and Comprehension
(Item from Fifth Grade Level)

FIG. 7.1   A story written for fifth grade children in Chinese and its English translation.

Pronunciation and Meaning

A third misconception about the Chinese writing system is that each character can be broken down into two parts, one revealing information about pronunciation and the other yielding information about meaning. For example,
in the character 桐 the left radical (the signific) stands for "tree" and gives
us a clue that the character might represent a type of tree. However, this is a
very general piece of information; scores of characters contain this radical,
and each represents something having to do with trees or wood. Similarly,
radicals such as 氵, which denotes water, or 金, which appears in characters
concerned with metals, again pertain to very broad categories that give only
vague cues about meaning.

The right component (the phonetic) of the character provides information
about pronunciation. The character 桐 is pronounced "tong." In this case
the right-hand component 同 also is pronounced "tong." Unfortunately, this
type of aid to pronunciation occurs only in a limited number of characters.
This can be illustrated with the character 柏 . Here, the pronunciation of
the right component is "bai." The pronunciation of the character, however, is
"bou." "Bou" is the ancient pronunciation of the right component. Thus,
even though in this case the right component carries information about pronunciation, the information is of little value to the contemporary reader. In
other cases there is no relation between the pronunciation of the right component and the pronunciation of the character. For example, the left hand
portion of the character 信 means person ("ren") and the right hand portion
means word ("yen"). The pronunciation of the whole character, however, is
"xing."

Thus, we are not necessarily given cues about pronunciation from the components of the character, and only in some cases can we deduce meaning
from the contribution of elements within or between characters. Learning
one meaning and one pronunciation for a character is only the beginning. A
much more complex, rich, and subtle set of meanings must be acquired in order to be a skilled reader of Chinese. As the writing system has evolved over
thousands of years, the relation between script and idea in written Chinese
has become increasingly complicated.

Phonetic Recoding

Another important error is to assume that the reader of Chinese derives
meaning directly from the perceptual characteristics of characters without re-
course to phonetic recoding. Research has suggested that visual processing of
both Chinese characters and English words does involve phonetic recoding
(Treiman, Baron, & Luk, 1981; Tzeng, Hung, & Wang, 1977). We can illustrate this point by briefly reviewing a typical study. In Tzeng, Hung, and

Wang's (1977) research, for example, sets of four Chinese characters were presented to Chinese subjects, followed by six other characters representing words that contained the same beginning consonant, the same terminal vowel, or the same consonant and the same vowel as in the first group of characters. The characters in the third case had the same pronunciation as the original characters and differed only according to one of the four tones of Mandarin Chinese. The original list was presented visually and the interference lists, aurally. Strong interference effects appeared in the recall of the original list of characters, especially when the pronunciation of the characters in the original and interference lists shared a common vowel or both a consonant and a vowel. Had the original characters been read solely according to meaning, there would have been little basis for a differential effect of the intervening materials upon their retention. Results such as these cast great doubt on the proposal that, in reading Chinese characters, meaning emerges directly from perception.

Teaching Children to Read Chinese

The major problems faced by teachers in Chinese elementary schools are to get the children to pronounce the characters correctly and to gain meaning from the characters. The approaches used in teaching differ, depending upon where the teaching occurs. Different systems are used in Hong Kong, Taiwan, and the People's Republic of China. In Hong Kong, characters are introduced with no aids to pronunciation. Characters are pronounced for the child, their meaning is explained, and the children are expected to remember what they have been told. In Taiwan, *zhuyin fuhao,* a phonetic spelling system, is used to assist the child in pronouncing characters. *Zhuyin fuhao* is a set of 37 symbols for which there is consistent grapheme-phoneme correspondence. The pronunciation of any Chinese character can be represented by no more than three of these symbols. In the People's Republic of China, *pinyin,* an alphabetic form of writing with consistent grapheme-phoneme correspondence, has been adopted for this purpose. Markers indicating the four tones of Mandarin Chinese are further aids to pronunciation.

It is a surprise to most visitors in Chinese first-grade classrooms to see that characters are not introduced until after the children have received 8 or so weeks of instruction with *zhuyin fuhao* or *pinyin. Zhuyin fuhao* notation continues to be printed alongside all characters in the reading textbooks in Taiwan for the first several years of elementary school. It is then used primarily for teaching new characters but no longer appears printed alongside characters that already have been introduced. *Pinyin* is rapidly displaced, except for new or especially difficult characters. Examples of the three approaches to teaching characters appear in Fig. 7.2.

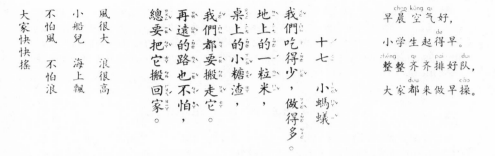

FIG. 7.2 Examples from first-grade reading texts used in Hong Kong, Taiwan, and the People's Republic of China. *Zhuyin fuhao* notation is on the right of each of the characters in the Taiwan texts and *pinyin* appears above new or difficult characters in the text from the People's Republic of China.

Teachers introduce several characters each day, and through successive years of elementary school, children's reading vocabularies increase. By the end of the sixth grade, they have acquired the approximately 3000 characters needed for reasonable literacy. Although, initially, the meaning of combinations of characters must be memorized, consistencies in their use sometimes make it easier for the experienced reader to learn the meaning and pronunciation of new words employing one or more of these characters. For example, after the Chinese child has learned that the character 國 (guo) means country, 民 (min) means person, 旗 (chi) means flag, and 寶 (bao) means treasure, it is relatively easy to learn that 國 民 (guo-min) means a citizen, 國 旗 (guo-chi) means the national flag, and that the characters 國 寶 (guo-bao) mean a national treasure.

Need for Research

Many of the arguments about the strengths and weaknesses of various orthographic systems have been based not only on an incomplete understanding of the various writing systems, but on a striking paucity of information. Little is known about the relative rates at which children acquire skill in reading languages such as Chinese and English, or about the kinds of skills and experiences that may be related to early progress in reading different orthographic systems. The literature on learning to read English is voluminous, and there are numerous studies on learning how to read Chinese. But comparative studies involving young Chinese- and English-speaking children are nearly impossible to locate. One reason is that no instruments with similar content and comparable levels of difficulty have been available in both languages to make comparisons of the children's reading skill possible.

We recently undertook a large study concerned with this problem. Two of our goals were to (1) construct a reading test in Chinese and English that would be suitable for elementary school children, and (2) investigate factors such as cognitive skills that might be related to progress in reading during the first months of children's attendance at school.

DEVELOPING THE READING TEST

We devised a reading test that contained three types of items: sight reading of vocabulary, reading of meaningful text material, and comprehension of text. Constructing such a test was an arduous task. We began by compiling lists of all vocabulary words introduced in Chinese, Japanese, and American elementary school textbooks. (Although data from Japan are not discussed in this paper, our study involved these three countries.) For this purpose we selected the current editions of two of the most popular text series in the United States and the single series used in Taiwan. Lists were created by entering words in English and transliterations of Chinese in *pinyin* into the computer. Accompanying each word were the grade and semester of its first appearance, the number of characters in the Chinese word, and the English translation. On completion, our lexicon contained approximately 21,000 computer entries, nearly evenly divided among the three languages. By the end of the sixth grade, therefore, children reading each language had encountered approximately 7000 words — a clear indication that the number of words learned by the Chinese children far exceeded the number of single characters they had been taught.

This information enabled us to include words in the reading test that were comparable across the three languages according to reading level. Preparation also included summarizing all the stories in the texts and identifying the grades at which various grammatical structures appeared. With this information, we were able to construct relevant items of comparable difficulty and equivalent grammatical complexity.

Items for the test were constructed simultaneously in all three languages, thereby avoiding the common practice of writing in one language and then translating the product into the other languages. Decisions about the acceptability of items were made through group discussion by persons from each culture who were familiar with at least two of the languages. All items were reviewed by professionals in each culture to insure that the items were culturally appropriate, written in standard forms of the language, and were satisfactory for children of the ages included in our study.

The test was composed of four parts arranged according to grade level:

Kindergarten Items.   The kindergarten test involved matching, naming, and identifying letters in English and *zhuyin fuhao* in Chinese.

Vocabulary. The vocabulary portion of the test was designed to assess the child's ability to sight-read single isolated words. In grades one to three the words were common to all three languages, but in grades four to six there were insufficient new vocabulary items common to the three languages. It was necessary, therefore, to use different words in the three forms of the test at grades four to six. To insure comparability, words selected for the test at grades four to six appeared for the first time at a particular grade level and had a similar frequency of usage as determined by reference to frequency counts of words in English and of characters in Chinese. The vocabulary portion of the test contained 61 words.

Reading and Comprehending Text. These portions of the test provided indices of the child's ability to read meaningful text presented in clauses, sentences, and paragraphs and to respond to true-false and multiple-choice questions. Three types of items were included: (a) phrases or sentences describing one of three pictures; (b) sentences in which certain key words were omitted, but for which three alternatives were available; and (c) paragraphs about which questions were asked. The child was asked to read the item and then choose the correct picture or alternative.

Examples of items in the four portions of the test are in Fig. 7.3. There were separate booklets for each language; items from the Chinese and English versions have been combined in this figure for purposes of illustration.

Scoring the Test

Three scores corresponded to the three parts of the text (excluding the kindergarten part):

The *vocabulary score* was the number of vocabulary items read correctly. If a Chinese vocabulary item was composed of more than a single character, all characters had to be read correctly in order for the item to be considered correct.

The *text-reading score* in English was the proportion of all words in the text that were read correctly. Since it is not always clear what constitutes a word in Chinese text, we computed the percentage of single characters that were read correctly.

The *comprehension score* was the number of correct alternatives chosen in multiple-choice and true-false items evaluating the children's understanding of what they read.

Administering the Test

The reading test was administered approximately 4 months after the children entered the first grade. The test was given individually to each child by examiners who were residents of the cities in which the children lived.

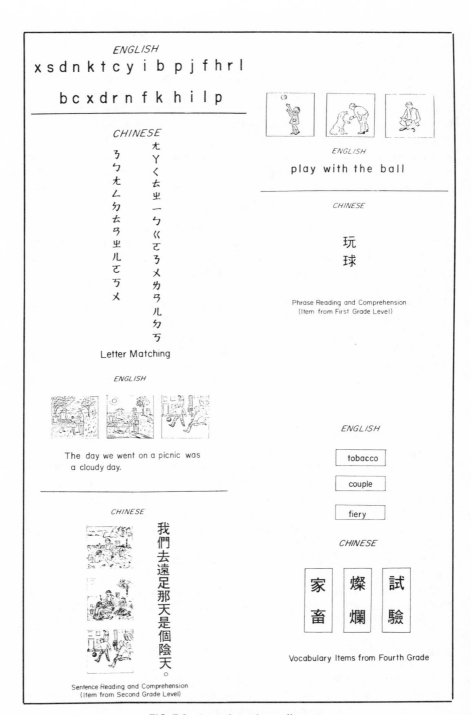

FIG. 7.3 Items from the reading text.

Intercorrelation of Reading Subscores

The three portions of the test were highly interrelated, and the correlations were similar for the Chinese and American versions of the test. Intercorrelations among the three scores ranged from .83 to .96. The coefficient of concordance for the Chinese version of the test was .91, and for the American version, .94. It is apparent from these values that the test is highly reliable.

All children began at the kindergarten level of the test. If the child was unable to read more than one vocabulary item correctly or if incorrect answers were given to four consecutive comprehension items at grade 1, the child was asked to stop after finishing all the first-grade items. Thus, complete scores for the grade 1 level were available for all children. If the criteria for stopping were not met, testing was continued. Items at the successive grade levels were presented until the child reached a point where fewer than three-fourths of the items at a grade level were passed. Once testing at a grade level began, all items at that grade level were presented.

Cognitive Tasks

Ten cognitive tasks were constructed for the study and were administered individually to the children approximately 3 months after the reading test. Tasks were selected on the basis of either a hypothesized differential relation to reading ability in the three languages or prior research in which similar tasks had been found to be related to reading ability.

Coding. A timed coding task was used in which the figures capitalized on the detection of spatial differences involving up-down, left-right relations, dimensions of difference often believed to produce problems in reading English.

Spatial Relations and Perceptual Speed. These two tasks, both of which use geometrical figures, were adapted from the Thurstone Primary Mental Abilities Battery. It was assumed that performance on these tasks would be more closely related to reading Chinese characters, where spatial ability and ability to recognize small details of difference are presumably more important than in reading English, which involves recombinatons of a relatively small number of letters.

Auditory Memory. Many have suggested that memory for auditory sequences may be related to reading English. Because of differences between Chinese and American children in their experience with musical and speech tones and other auditory material, a task was constructed in which the child was required to remember patterns of atonal sequences of different duration.

Serial Memory for Words and Numbers.   Words were selected from the children's readers and were reviewed by native speakers for their relevance and usefulness. The numbers were selected at random.

Verbal-spatial Representation.   This task of 13 items was an adaptation and extension of an earlier task constructed by Yung-ho Ko, Professor of Psychology at National Taiwan University. Professor Ko has found a positive relation between the rate at which children learn Chinese characters and their ability to follow verbal directions in drawing figures with differing spatial arrangements.

Verbal Memory.   Many Wetern studies have found that memory for text is a significant predictor of reading ability. The story written for this task was judged by Chinese and American colleagues to be culturally fair and linguistically comparable.

Vocabulary.   Items were obtained for consideration from the Chinese, Japanese, and American versions of the Wechsler Intelligence Scale for Children, from our computer lexicon, and from popular books and magazines from each country. The test contained 25 items.

General Information.   A distinction was made between items tapping inferential reasoning and common information. It was decided to minimize the number of the first type inasmuch as the purpose of the test was to assess the amount of common knowledge the child had accumulated through everyday experience. There were 26 items.

SUBJECTS

The subjects were first-grade children from the Minneapolis and Taipei metropolitan areas. These cities were chosen because of their comparable size and cultural characteristics within each country. Ten schools were randomly selected to represent the range of its schools. Two first-grade classes were then chosen at random within each school.

Because of differences in class size, 410 children were enrolled in the 20 classes in Minneapolis, and 912 children in the 20 classrooms in Taipei. The mean age of the Chinese children at the time of testing was 81.1 months and for the American children, 83.1 months. All mentally retarded children were eliminated in Taipei on the basis of scores on the Raven's Colored Progressive Matrices Test. All Minneapolis children suspected of mental retardation had been tested in kindergarten or at the beginning of first grade and were enrolled in special classes.

The cognitive tasks could not be given to all children in each class because of limitations in time and funds. Therefore, these tasks were administered to a representative sample of 240 children, which included six boys and six girls selected from each of the 20 classrooms in each city. Two boys and two girls were randomly chosen from the upper, middle, and lower third of the distribution of reading scores within each classroom.

READING SCORES

The overall scores of the children on the reading test appear in Figs. 7.4, 7.5 and 7.6. For the vocabulary and reading comprehension scores, the proportions of children are plotted according to the number of correct responses made on the test. For reading of text, the proportions are plotted according to the percentage of words or characters read correctly. The Chinese children received higher scores than the American children on both comprehension and reading of text (Scheffe contrasts, $p < .01$). There was no significant difference between the two groups of children in the average number of vocabulary items read correctly.

For the items that appeared only at grade 1, differences were significant for all three scores. The Chinese children not only read and understood text at grade 1 better than the American children, but they also were able to read

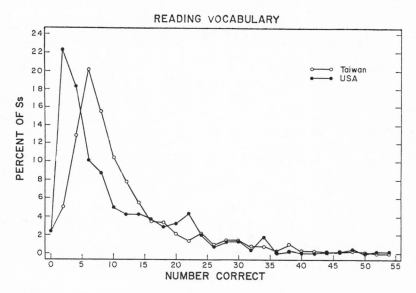

FIG. 7.4   Percent of subjects receiving each score on vocabulary items of the reading text.

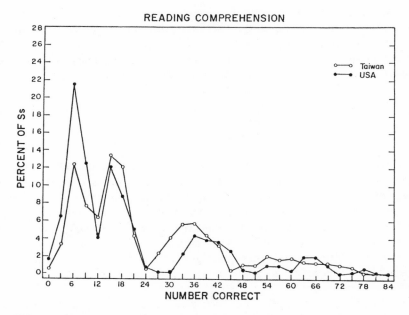

FIG. 7.5 Percent of subjects receiving each score on reading comprehension items.

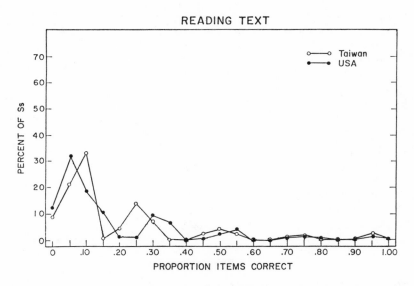

FIG. 7.6 Percent of subjects at each level of skill in reading meaningful text.

isolated words in the vocabulary test more effectively. The lack of a significant difference for the total vocabulary scores was due, therefore, to especially high scores received by some of the American children.

There were no significant sex differences in the scores for the Chinese children, but the American girls received higher scores than the American boys on all three portions of the test, $Fs > 9.60$, $p < .01$.

A second index of the children's reading ability is the percentage of children who met the criteria to continue to the second grade level and beyond. Among the American children, 43% completed only the grade 1 level, 29% advanced to the grade 2 level, and 28% continued to the grade 3 level and beyond. Among the Chinese children, the corresponding percentages were 23% (grade 1), 37% (grade 2), and 40% (grade 3 and beyond).

Among the children who were unable to advance further than the first grade, the Chinese children received significantly higher scores than the American children, $p < .01$. On the other hand, among the children who were able to go beyond the second grade level, vocabulary scores of the American children significantly surpassed those of the Chinese children $p < .001$. Among these advanced readers, scores also were higher for reading text and reading comprehension among the American than among the Chinese children, but the differences were not statistically significant. Figure 7.7 presents these data, along with the percentages of children who were able to go on to grade levels 4, 5, and 6. It is evident that there were first-grade children in both cities who were reading at the sixth grade level.

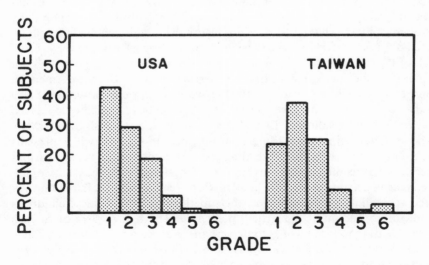

FIG. 7.7   Percentage of American and Chinese children completing each level of the reading test.

We can use the data from the Japanese, as well as the Chinese and American children, to construct a final index of reading ability. This index results from selecting the 100 children who received the highest scores and the 100 children who received the lowest scores from among the 2111 Chinese, Japanese, and American first graders who were administered the reading test. Among the 100 children who received the lowest vocabulary scores, ten were Chinese and 47 were American. Among the 100 who received the lowest scores in reading comprehension, 35 were Chinese and 56 were American. Of the 100 children who received the highest vocabulary scores, 40 were Chinese and 47 were American. In reading comprehension, 43 of the top 100 readers were Chinese and 32 were American. With one exception, therefore, these scores also indicate a superiority in the reading ability of the Chinese children.

Whatever index we use, the general tendency is for Chinese first-graders to surpass American first-graders in reading skill. This finding would be predicted on the basis of some of the positions discussed at the beginning of this paper. However, before we can assume that Chinese characters are easier for the beginning reader to learn than are English words, we must look briefly at the results for the Japanese children. In the early grades the vocabulary items of the Japanese version of the test were identical to those of the Chinese version. Japanese *kanji* are Chinese characters to which Japanese readings are given. The average number of vocabulary items written in *kanji* that were read correctly by the Japanese first-grade children was 6.7. The Chinese children read an average of 10.3 of these items correctly, and the American children an average of 9.4 of the corresponding English words. An orthography involving Chinese characters does not insure that children will read well.

In addition, several points can be made about English orthography. First, lack of knowledge of the elements of the writing system in English does not explain the poor performance of the American children. Even the American children who could not read past the first-grade level were correct on 98.4% of the items at the kindergarten level, which, it will be remembered, involved recognition and reading of English letters. Nor does English orthography *necessarily* result in poor reading. This is evident in Fig. 7.8, which presents the average raw scores on the reading test for children who were at various percentiles of reading ability. In the comprehension of text, the Chinese children received higher raw scores at all levels of reading ability. In reading isolated vocabulary items, however, the superiority of the Chinese children's scores disappears after the fiftieth percentile. The best readers of English were able to read more words than were the best readers of Chinese. These advanced readers of English appeared to benefit from the use of an alphabetical system. It is nearly impossible to guess the pronunciation or deduce the meaning of Chinese characters if the character has not been taught. In English, however, children can "sound out" new words. If the child knows the

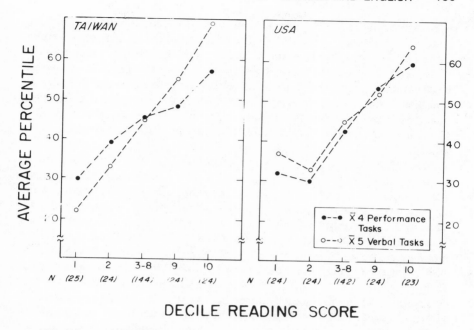

FIG. 7.8   Average percentile scores on verbal and performance tasks of children at various levels of reading skill.

meaning of the word sounded out in this fashion, the text can be understood. An impediment to Chinese children's utilizing this procedure is that they cannot guess the pronunciation. Even if they could, the large number of homophones in Chinese hampers the transition from hearing the sound to understanding the meaning of the word. Thus, the English-speaking child who has caught on to the system of breaking down the word into its constituent sounds has an advantage over the Chinese-speaking child who must depend upon some external source in order to acquire both the sound and meaning of the word.

Poor Readers

The superior performance of the Chinese first graders may lead to the erroneous conclusion that severe reading problems do not exist among children learning to read Chinese. This is a common belief (e.g., Taylor & Taylor, 1983), but one that is based on informal surveys rather than on the results of reading tests given to individual children. First graders with reading disabilities are difficult to detect. However, in the major study on which this research is based, half of the subjects were first graders and half were fifth graders. We will briefly look at some of the results for the fifth graders.

All the fifth graders were started on the fifth-grade items of the reading test. If they were not successful on three-fourths of these items, they were required to go to the fourth grade items. If they were not successful on ¾ of these items they were required to go to the third-grade items. In this way a child could be forced to go back as far as the first grade. The results indicated that 3% of the Chinese children and 3.5% of the American children failed to meet the criteria for success at grade 3 and were therefore reading at least three years below their grade level—a common criterion for reading disability.

In Fig. 7.9, the scores at each grade level of the test are presented according to the children's level of reading ability. Looking first at the hatched line, we see that the fifth-grade items of the test were effective in separating the various levels of reading ability; children who eventually were required to go back to the first- or second-grade levels received lower scores than those who went back to the third-grade level, and so forth. The same kind of hierarchy emerged for items at each grade level of the test. Vocabulary scores were higher for the Chinese than for the American children at each reading level except in the case of the worst readers—children who were tested with first- or second-grade items. These children had the worst reading vocabularies of all the children. Reading comprehension scores at various levels of reading ability are more similar between the two groups of children. Even here, however, Chinese children who were poor readers received scores as low or lower than those obtained by the American children at all levels of the test. There is no support in these data for arguments that the holistic perception of distinctive Chinese characters precludes the appearance of severe problems in learning to read.

THE SEARCH FOR EXPLANATIONS

The search for an adequate explanation of our findings is a long one, for many factors are involved in producing differences in reading skill between Chinese and American first graders. For our purposes here, some of the most obvious alternatives are discussed, including parent education, cognitive ability, and several factors related to school and home.

Educational Status of the Parents

Parents' educational status typically is found to be related to children's levels of achievement within a culture. Thus, it might be suspected that the Chinese families included in our sample exceeded the American families in their educational status. This was not the case. Only 6% of the American parents, but 61% of the Chinese parents, had less than a high school education. Over

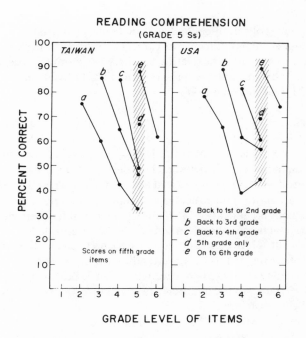

READING COMPREHENSION
(GRADE 5 Ss)

TAIWAN   USA

PERCENT CORRECT

a Back to 1st or 2nd grade
b Back to 3rd grade
c Back to 4th grade
d 5th grade only
e On to 6th grade

Scores on fifth grade items

GRADE LEVEL OF ITEMS

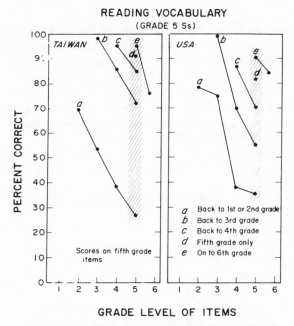

READING VOCABULARY
(GRADE 5 Ss)

TAIWAN   USA

PERCENT CORRECT

a Back to 1st or 2nd grade
b Back to 3rd grade
c Back to 4th grade
d Fifth grade only
e On to 6th grade

Scores on fifth grade items

GRADE LEVEL OF ITEMS

FIG. 7.9 Raw scores at each level of the vocabulary and comprehension items of the reading test plotted according to children's level of reading ability.

half the Minneapolis mothers had attended college or graduate school, a figure much higher than that found in Taipei (12.8%). Within each group, however, there was a significant relationship between parents' educational status and children's overall scores on the reading test. In Minneapolis the correlation was .33, and in Taipei, .26.

Teachers

Another possibility is that the training teachers received contributed to their pupils' academic success. However, the American teachers were all university or college graduates. One-fourth had a master's degree, and one had a Ph.D. Nearly all had majored in education as undergraduates; 76 percent had majored in elementary education. In Taiwan, nearly all teachers were graduates of five-year teachers' colleges in which they had enrolled after graduating from middle school. In contrast to the American teachers, the Taipei teachers began their teaching careers after attending the equivalent of three years of high school and two years of college. There is little basis for explaining cross-national differences in the children's performance in terms of the amount of training of their teachers.

Children's Cognitive Level

A positive relation between the children's cognitive level and their academic achievement is commonly reported. Perhaps the Chinese children simply were brighter than the American children and thus learned more rapidly. No evidence was found to support this interpretation. There were no significant differences between the two sets of scores on three of the cognitive tests (coding, spatial relations, and memory for words); the Chinese children received significantly higher scores on serial memory for numbers, but the American first graders received significantly higher scores on the remaining tests (perceptual speed, auditory memory, general information, vocabulary, verbal memory, and verbal-spatial representation).

Relation of Cognitive Variables and Reading Scores

As we indicated earlier, the cognitive tasks were selected for several purposes, one of which was to assess their possible differential relation to reading ability in the two writing systems. Cues about possible bases of difference in the children's performance on the reading task may be found in an examination of these relationships. For this purpose, regression analyses predicting children's reading scores were conducted in which the entries were the scores on the ten cognitive tasks and a summary score combining the three components of the reading test. Results of the analyses for the Chinese and American children were similar. The multiple correlation for the Chinese sample was .60, and for the American sample, .62. Tasks that contributed significantly, $p < .05$, to both multiple correlations were general information, verbal-spatial representations, and spatial relations. Two tasks entered significantly into the multiple correlation for the American, but not for the Chinese children: auditory memory and coding. The converse was found for two tasks. Verbal memory and serial memory for numbers made significant independent contributions to the multiple correlation for the Chinese, but not for the American children. A summary of the step-wise regression analysis is presented in Table 7.1.

The cognitive tasks were not especially revealing, therefore, of differential abilities that might be involved in reading Chinese and in reading English. As expected, auditory memory and coding were more strongly related to reading English than Chinese, but spatial relations and verbal-spatial representation, which we predicted would be more strongly related to early reading in Chinese than in English, were equally related to reading skill in both writing systems.

A different perspective on the relation of the cognitive tasks to reading emerges when the tasks are grouped into verbal and performance tasks. Five tasks relied on verbal response: serial memory for words and numbers, verbal memory, vocabulary, and general information. There were four perform-

TABLE 7.1
Summary of the Stepwise Regression Analyses Relating Cognitive
Tasks to Reading Scores

Task	Partial r	R^2	p
United States			
Verbal-spatial representation	.47	.22	.01
General information	.31	.29	.01
Auditory memory	.25	.34	.01
Coding	.21	.37	.05
Spatial relations	.16	.38	.05
Taiwan			
General information	.51	.26	.001
Verbal memory	.26	.31	.05
Verbal-spatial representation	.18	.33	.05
Serial memory for numbers	.15	.34	.05
Spatial relations	.13	.36	.05

ance tasks: coding, spatial relations, perceptual speed, and auditory memory. The tenth task, verbal-spatial representation, involved a verbal stimulus and a nonverbal response. Average percentiles for the scores received on the verbal and on the performance tasks were computed for the children in each country according to the decile into which their reading scores fell. These data are plotted in Fig. 7.10. The curves for the Chinese and American children are similar for the performance tasks but different for the verbal tasks. Scores on the verbal tasks provide a clearer differentiation between the various levels of reading ability among the Chinese than among the American children. In other words, verbal and performance tasks contributed more equally to level of reading ability among the readers of English, but verbal tasks made a greater contribution than did the performance tasks to the level of reading ability among the readers of Chinese. This statement is supported statistically by the results of a LISREL analysis in which there was greater equivalence in the factor loadings of verbal and performance tasks for the American than for the Chinese children. The standardized factor loadings of verbal and performance tasks on reading for the American children were 1.52

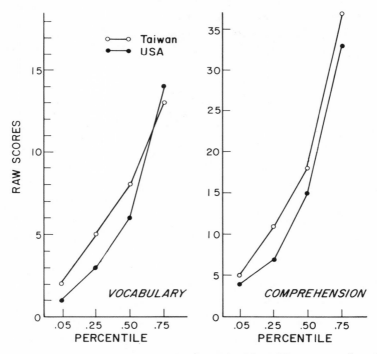

FIG. 7.10   Vocabulary and comprehension scores plotted according to percentile on the reading test.

for verbal and 1.32 for performance tasks. The comparable loadings for the Chinese children were 1.52 and .35.

In summary, we did not uncover any cognitive factors that lead one to be especially pessimistic about English orthography. There are some interesting indications that verbal and performance tasks may have different significance in reading Chinese and English, but further research will be needed to clarify how such differences might operate. Our results suggest that children do poorly in reading English, not because their cognitive abilities are below those of Chinese children, but because of other factors.

SCHOOL VARIABLES

Time Spent in Reading Classes

One variable that logically might be related to degree of learning is the amount of time spent in practice. We looked, therefore, at the children's activities at school. Children in Taipei attend school for approximately 240 days each year. In contrast, the American school year typically includes only 178 days of instruction. Overall, therefore, the Chinese children had received many more hours of instruction prior to taking the reading test than had the American children.

We are able to provide a detailed analysis of how the children spent their time in school. Among the many variables coded in observations made in the children's classrooms, one was the subject being taught. The first-grade children in Taipei were observed for 800 hours and the American children, for over 650 hours. Since the observational periods were randomly assigned, highly reliable estimates of the proportion of time spent in being taught various subjects can be obtained.

As can be seen in Fig. 7.11, the proportion of time spent on language, mathematics, social science, music, art, moral education, and other subjects appears to be similar in the first-grade Chinese and American classrooms. But spending time in a class does not necessarily mean that the children will learn. We found strong evidence that the Chinese children were much more likely to attend to the teacher and their work than were the American children. This is evident in Fig. 7.12, in which the percentage of time spent in irrelevant activities is presented. An activity was coded as being inappropriate when the child was not doing what he or she was expected or supposed to be doing. This included such activities as talking to peers, asking inappropriate or irrelevant questions, and wandering about the room. A much greater portion of class time was spent by American children than by Chinese children in activities that interfere with learning.

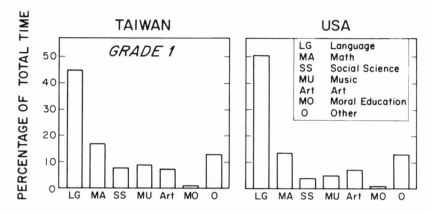

FIG. 7.11   Proportions of time spent on various academic subjects.

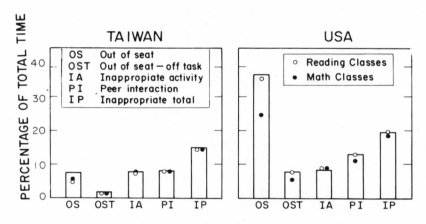

FIG. 7.12   Percentage of time spent in various types of irrelevant activities.

Homework

Learning also occurs at home. Part of the learning at home takes place as children practice their lessons through homework. From responses made by the American parents and teachers, we have many indications that neither group considers homework to be of great value. This attitude is in marked contrast with that of Chinese parents and teachers. As a consequence, American children spent vastly less time in homework than did Chinese children.

One indication of the amount of time children spent doing homework comes from the estimates made by the children's mothers, who were asked how much time their children typically spent on homework each weekday and during each day of the weekend. In Fig. 7.13 are z scores derived from a distribution of the mothers' estimates of the total amount of time their children spent in homework during the preceding week. (To compute the z scores, the data for Chinese, Japanese, and American first graders were combined into one distribution. The resulting z scores were then recombined according to the children's classrooms.) The height of the line in Fig. 7.12, represents the average for the classroom, and the length of the line represents the distance covered by the mean ±3 SD. The differences between the Chinese and American estimates are enormous. There is great homogeneity in the estimates by the mothers of the American children within each classroom, and a greater range in the estimates made by the mothers of the Chinese children within each classroom. Overall, the American first graders were estimated to spend an average of 14 minutes a day on weekdays, 3 minutes on Saturday, and 4 minutes on Sunday on homework. The corresponding estimate for the Chinese children were 77 minutes (each weekday), 66 minutes (Saturday), and 42 minutes (Sunday).

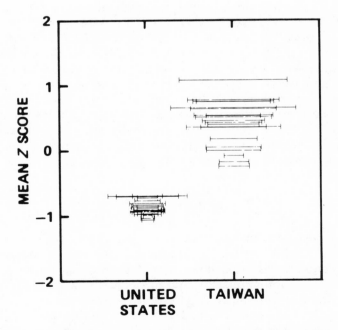

FIG. 7.13   Mothers' estimates of the amounts of time children spend doing homework, plotted according to classroom.

Parental Beliefs

Experiences provided by parents undoubtedly have a strong influence on children's academic achievement. These experiences, in turn, are influenced by the parents' beliefs about how successful their children are in school. If parents are satisfied with their children's performance, it is unlikely that they will demand that their children work harder on academic tasks. If they are not satisfied, there is impetus for them to attempt to remedy this situation by giving greater emphasis to the children's school work.

When asked about their child's current academic performance, few Chinese mothers indicated they were "very satisfied." Even though their children performed less well, American mothers were very positive. More than 40% of the American mothers described themselves as being "very satisfied." Nearly a third of the Chinese mothers said they were "not satisfied" with their children's performance, but only one in ten American mothers expressed such dissatisfaction.

American mothers also were very pleased with the job the schools were doing in educating their children. The mothers were asked, "How good a job would you say _____'s school is doing this year in educating _____?" Among American mothers, 91% judged the school was doing an "excellent" or "good" job. Only 42% of the Chinese mothers were this positive. Instead, the majority of the Chinese mothers considered that the schools were doing a "fair" job. Nor did American mothers express any dissatisfaction with the level of difficulty of the school curriculum. Mothers in both cities strongly believed that the curricula of their children's schools were about right: 89% of the American mothers and 83% of the Chinese mothers.

These data pose an interesting paradox. American mothers were more positive than the Chinese mothers about their children's scholastic experiences and progress. At the same time, the American children generally demonstrated lower levels of achievement in reading.

CONCLUSIONS

We have a great deal more information about correlates of learning to read Chinese and English, but there is insufficient space here to consider them. From what we have discussed, however, we find little evidence that orthography is a major basis for explaining the superior performance of Chinese children. Learning to read Chinese requires much more complex cognitive activity than earlier discussions of the relation between orthography and reading imply. It is not a result of rote paired-associate learning of the sound and meaning of several thousand symbols, each standing for a single word. There has been a continuous development of the Chinese writing system as it became necessary to represent increasingly abstract ideas.

Children may encounter some problems in learning to read that are related to orthography, but other factors appear to play a more critical role. We have described several of these. It is no surprise to find American children doing less well than the Chinese children when we also find that they spend less time in school, they spend less time attending to their work while in school, and spend less time doing homework out of school. American parents do not provide the impetus for their children to work harder, for they are more satisfied than are Chinese parents with their children's academic achievement and with the job the schools are doing. We conclude, therefore, that some of the most critical reasons Chinese children learn to read efficiently and with comprehension are because they work hard at the task and because they receive encouragement from both teachers and parents, who are dedicated to the continuous improvement of the children's education.

ACKNOWLEDGMENTS

The research project in which data discussed in this paper were collected has involved collaboration with Professors G. William Lucker of the University of Texas (El Paso); C. C. Hsu of Taiwan National University, Taipei; Seiro Kitamura of Tohoku Fukushi College, Sendai, Japan. The research is supported by a grant from the National Institute of Mental Health (Grant MH 31567).

REFERENCES

Gleitman, L. R., & Rozin, P. (1977). The structure and acquisition of reading I: Relation between orthographies and the structure of language. In A. S. Reber & D. L. Scarborough (Eds.), *Toward a psychology of reading.* (pp. 1–50). Hillsdale, NJ: Lawrence Erlbaum Associates.

Hatano, G., Kuhara, K., & Akiyama, M. (1981). Kanji help readers of Japanese infer the meaning of unfamiliar words. *The Quarterly Newsletter of the Laboratory of Comparative Human Cognition 3,* 30–33.

Martin, S. E. (1972). Nonalphabetic writing systems. In J. F. Kavanagh & I. G. Mattingly (Eds.), *Language by ear and by eye. The relationships between speech and reading.* (pp. 81–102). Cambridge, MA: MIT Press.

Rozin, P., & Gleitman, L. R. (1977). The structure and acquisition of reading II: The reading process and the acquisition of the alphabetic principle. In A. S. Reber & D. L. Scarborough (Eds.), *Toward a psychology of reading.* (pp. 55–142). Hillsdale, NJ: Lawrence Erlbaum Associates.

Rozin, P., Porutsky, S., & Sotsky, R. (1973). American children with reading problems can easily learn to read English represented by Chinese characters. In F. Smith (Ed.), *Psycholinguistics and reading.* (pp. 105–115). N.Y.: Holt, Rinehart & Winston.

Taylor, I., & Taylor, M. M. (1983). *The psychology of reading.* N.Y.: Academic.

Treitman, R. A., Baron, J., & Luk, K. (1981). Speech recoding in silent reading: A comparison of Chinese and English. *Journal of Chinese Linguistics, 9,* 116–125.

Tzeng, O., Hung, D. L., & Wang, S. Y. (1977). Speech recoding in reading Chinese characters. *Journal of Experimental Psychology: Human Learning and Memory, 3,* 621–630.

8 The Reading Achievement Game: Cognitive Universals and Cultural Constraints

Alexander W. Siegel
University of Houston

Introductory Remarks

I feel a bit uneasy making lengthy comments about topics with which I have really little *actual* experience. I've neither conducted nor published any research on reading, and I've read only enough about cross-cultural research to be slightly dangerous. Consequently, I will not present any new data or directions for future research (a common topic in such "commentaries").

Nonetheless, I am writing this "discussion" for several reasons. First, I am one of the book's editors (and was one of the conference organizers). Nearly a year ago Barbara Foorman had an idea for a conference on reading and asked if I would be interested in organizing it with her. I was — and did. But I didn't know what I was *really* getting into.

Second, although I've done a good deal of research on cognitive development, only in the last several years have I really begun to see and understand and write about how most cognitive activities are fundamentally social, i.e., they take place in a set of nested social contexts. I view a good piece of what has been called cognitive development as consisting of the child's growing competence with symbol systems for the purpose of communicating and cooperating at a distance. Much of what children are taught in school — as a function of what society demands of its schools — is what White (1978) has called "public thinking." In large measure, such public thinking involves (1) competence and habitual use of symbol systems designed for communication with others distal in time and space; (2) mastery of the conceptual forms of adult society (e.g., dimensionalization and metricization of experience, spatial and temporal conventions, etc.); and (3) mastery of the social forms of adult society (e.g., evaluations, styles and etiquettes of communication, etc.). Reading and learning to read then, are of interest to me because of both their cognitive and their social implications.

A third reason for being a discussant is more personal. (Although this formal discussion is directed towards the paper by Lee, Stigler, and Stevenson in this volume, much of what I will have to say was stimulated by Harold Stevenson's presentation — somewhat broader in scope than the formal paper — at the conference itself.) Harold Stevenson was my advisor, mentor, friend, and father-figure while I was a graduate student at the Institute of Child Development at the University of Minnesota back in the 1960s. Harold was the Director of the Institute and had an active, vibrant, and productive research program. During my second year, he took me under his wing, and we worked closely for the next three years. Talk about an education! Harold taught me how to do research, he was my model for a professional, and he taught me how to survive professionally, i.e., publish. This conference is the first occasion at which I have had the opportunity to comment publically on his research. The opportunity is both welcome and, given my lack of expertise, also slightly scary.

Harold's paper exemplifies some of the principles (conveyed in action rather than speech; implicit, but very real) I picked up from him during those graduate school years. The first principle is, "Start with an interesting question." Harold appears to have gotten into reading initially because of the interesting, but then unsubstantiated, claims of clinicians and educators that reading disabilities were rare among Chinese and Japanese children. The initial question — Is this surprising claim valid? — is asked at a macro-, rather than a micro-, level of analysis.

Harold's second principle is, in the absence of any guiding theory, "Do something!" That is, get an empirical handle on the problem. Design a set of procedures that work. Design them as carefully and as rigorously as you can. The procedures don't have to be perfect, so don't wait for perfection. You can go a long way with an imperfect set of procedures and/or a partial theory. Harold and his collaborators have meticulously designed individually administered reading tests, mathematics tests, and tests of more general cognitive skills. They have developed observational schemes and parent and teacher rating instruments. Doing this well *within* a culture is difficult in and of itself. But designing procedures that are comparable — and one could quibble with little bits and pieces here and there about things that are not as comparable as one might like — across three *different* cultures is an empirical and logistical tour de force. Harold shows us the richness of a non-experimental approach in raising interesting questions, the subtlety of "interpretation" of cross-cultural data. In doing so, he downplays just how hard it is to do this kind of research.

Harold's paper makes it clear that if you take the first empirical step, you will open more doors and uncover more questions than you had anticipated — another principle. That is, your initial foray will uncover ways in which the macro-level aspects of the system, e.g., the culture, influence the target domain or skill. I don't think the research game is really about getting answers — timeless and spaceless truths (Siegel, 1981; White & Siegel, 1984). Rather, it's asking better questions and, from the data gleaned, taking a broader look (or in the case of experimental work, a more penetrating look), deriving timely and spaceful truths, posing options and possibilities that *perhaps,* in the hands of decision-makers, can be used to make better-informed judgments regarding educational policy affecting the daily lives of children.

Harold's deep involvement in the arena of child development and social policy has clearly influenced his current research. Historically, it's a very different kind of research than what he published from the 1950s to the 1970s. For the record, Harold — first at the University of Texas, then at the University of Minnesota — was a central figure in spearheading and nurturing what is now called "experimental child psychology." The early work was primarily experimental and of narrower scope. I cut my teeth on this kind of research. Although intellectually and procedurally rigorous, this kind of work is relatively circumscribed and "safe". It's a pretty big leap from these experimental data to statements about social policy, and a safe retreat is always "...more research is needed." When you get into the arena Harold has carved out for himself, you live a bit more dangerously. The leap from data to policy recommendations is fairly short, often obvious (though clearly value laden), and the retreat to "...more research is needed" is a less credible one in the public or Congressional eye. Doing this kind of research — laying it on the line like this — takes courage.

In the remainder of this discussion, I would like to address several questions aimed at a broader analysis of the social context of reading. Posed simplistically, these are (1) Why has Jeffrey learned to read? (2) Is Jeffrey reading less well or differently than his Chinese counterpart? (3) If so, what factors in the social context of learning to read might produce these differences?

Why has Jeffrey Learned to Read? Or, Why Reading is a Many-Layered Thing

The problem of causation in the study of psychological things — like reading — is clearly different from that in the study of physical things. It's more complex, because any psychological "thing" is multiply controlled at a number of different levels of anlaysis. I have adapted the following analysis of Why Jeffrey has learned to read in large measure from Sheldon White (1978).

1. Jeffrey has learned to read because a series of repeated translations from light-dark configurations in the visual field into patterned retinal firings have progressively established a set of presumptively biochemical changes in his nervous system.

2. He has learned to read because a series of eye movements have been integrated into organized sensorimotor routines, and because parallel and interactive routines involving auditory and articulatory processes have been established. These sight-sound-symbol correspondences permit him to decode and comprehend.

3. Jeffrey has learned to read because a series of postulated cognitive-psychological mechanisms have been—through maturation or training—sufficiently well developed. That is, Jeffrey has sufficient functional working memory and speed of lexical access (Perfetti, this volume), his schemata are sufficient such that text activates those schemata, and his world knowledge is sufficient to guide comprehension.

4. He has learned to read because he is motivated to learn to read. He wants to become part of adult society, so he puts in attention, effort, and intensity in the classroom, and this has brought him to reading.

5. Jeffrey has learned to read because his parents have, since preschool, led him to have faith in what reading can do. Often they have trained him in word identification, in the school years they have encouraged, allowed, and even forced him to attend school regularly.

6. Jeffrey has learned to read because his teacher—trained, experienced, and willing to exercise suitable routines of classroom management and organization—has offered him a set of experiences that have led him to read.

7. He has learned to read because the laws of his state require that all children must attend school after age six and be taught reading.

8. He has learned to read because the increased technological sophistication and increased development in his country has required that schools be created to provide literacy to all children.

9. Jeffrey has learned to read because the school board and taxpayers of his city have appropriated the funds with which to support the buildings and personnel of a school equipped to offer training in reading.

It is clear that, in this analysis, Jeffrey is a mythical creature—an average or aggregate child, not a flesh and blood child. But he is about as real as any other statistical entity we create, such as the mythical "average" 6-year-old (whose only common characteristic is astronomical—the earth has made six revolutions around the sun since the child was born). Yet, Jeffrey *is* real in that he concretizes an organism that can read.

I have just given you a list of nine different answers to the question of why Jeffrey has learned to read. They're all valid answers in the sense that they approach the "Why?" question with an acceptable form of a "because...." answer. One could generate more answers, but the point is that biochemists, optometrists, psychologists, parents, teachers, school administrators, politicians, and attorneys all have quite different interests in why Jeffrey has learned to read. Jeffrey is sitting there, and stretched out over his head is an immense multicausal apparatus of social control. People in the local school system and on the school board, in the state department of education, in the bureaucracy of DHHS are managing the whynesses of Jeffrey's reading: the whyness of teacher presence and competence, the whyness of parental willingness, of the law, of medical remediation of reading disabilities, etc. The fact that it takes a host of different people managing quite different things to get Jeffrey to read implies that we need a multiple knowledge base, pieces of which are represented in the research of all the authors in this volume. Different discourses need to be created. It is quite likely that the discourse that would help the parent may not be the discourse that would help the teacher or the school principal or the school superintendent or the Director of NIE or the Secretary of the Department of Education.

Is Jeffrey Reading Less Well or Differently Than His Chinese Counterpart?

Stevenson, Lee, Stigler, Kitamura, Kitamura, & Tadahisa (in press) found that the math achievement scores of American children were lower than those of Japanese and Chinese children. The picture for reading scores painted by Lee, Stigler, and Stevenson's current data in this volume is rather different. There are mean differences (p's $< .05$) for favoring Chinese over American readers in Comprehension (25.6, $SD = 18.7$ vs. 21.3, $SD = 18.2$) and Reading Text (% correct: .20, $SD = .21$ vs. .16, $SD = .18$), but not in Vocabulary (10.8, $SD = 9.1$ vs 10.0, $SD = 9.6$) (Stevenson, personal communication, January, 1985). There are also, certainly, differences in the form of the distribution of scores—American children seem to be over-represented at both the top and bottom portions of the distribution, both in decoding and comprehension at both first and fifth grades. Harold's data also seem to demonstrate that whatever performance differences exist are not due to differences in orthography or general cognitive ability. It certainly seems that the wider range and different form of the distribution of reading scores among American children reflects, in large measure, the diversity and plurality of American culture (including differences in values, aspirations, and parental and educational practices).

At this point, I would like to pose several questions. I have reservations about equating higher reading achievement scores with "reading well." If "reading well" means comprehension of new material through silent reading (the current standard of literacy in the U.S., Resnick & Resnick, 1977), do Harold's tests measure this? (Probably not at first grade, given our emphasis on "word-pronouncing.") Given some of the differences in educational and parental practices apparently favoring Chinese children, why are the American-Chinese mean differences in reading not larger than they are? What are some of the possible explanations for the differences in mean performance and in the range and form of the distributions between Chinese and American children?

What Are Some "Whys"?

(1.) The differences that exist do not seem to be due to biochemical or physiological differences, to differences in nervous system functioning, or to differences in basic cognitive abilities. Although some have argued for hardwired cultural differences in visual-spatial skills (involved in higher math), the evidence for cultural differences in visual- and phonological-analysis in children is nil. Further, as Lee et al.'s data indicate, the differences in reading achievement are not due to differences in intelligence or to other basic cognitive abilities.

(2.) I'm reasonably convinced that the different orthographies necessary in learning to read English vs. Chinese probably account for little of the variance in reading scores. Stevenson et al. (in press) provide evidence that Japanese children performed more poorly than American or Chinese children in reading vocabulary. Since the vocabulary words include Chinese characters for both Japanese and Chinese children, orthographic differences between Chinese logographs and the English alphabet do not seem to be important contributors to differences in reading achievement.

(3.) "Time-on-task" is an obvious candidate for one of the "whys" of American children's lower reading achievement scores. Lee et al.'s data indicate that American children receive about the same instruction in reading (more minutes per day, but for fewer days per year) and Stevenson et al. (in press) report that American children receive much less instruction in math (a good bit less per day for 33% fewer days per year). Given this, it is surprising that American children's math scores are not lower than they are! It's not just "time on task", but "effective time on task" that seems to be important. Here, American children get somewhat short shrift in reading and even shorter shrift in math. Further, Chinese children spend a good deal more time during the week and on weekends doing homework than do their American counterparts.

Harold's paper suggests potentially far more complex cultural influences on reading and mathematics achievement. Although differences in math scores (Stevenson et al., in press) could be largely accounted for by time-on-task, differences in the means and forms of distributions of reading scores seem to be attributable to other, less quantifiable factors.

(4.) What about motivation? It seems possible that the manner in which reading is taught in the early elementary school years in American schools —

primarily reading aloud, round-robin fashion, as an "exercise" in word-pronouncing rather than in meaning-getting—*decreases* rather than increases motivation, or perhaps makes it more variable. Further, it is possible that the content of most American elementary reading texts is sufficiently inane to make reading what Papert (1980) calls "dissociated learning." Thus, Jeffrey is turned off rather than turned on. A few quotes from Edmund Burke Huey's remarkable book, *The Psychology and Pedagogy of Reading,* seem as pertinent today as they did when written in 1908. In arguing that reading training should emphasize meaning-getting and silent reading Huey states:

> Reading as a school exercise has almost always been thought of as reading aloud, in spite of the obvious fact that reading in actual life is to be mainly silent reading. The consequent attention to reading as an exercise in speaking, and it has usually been a rather bad exercise in speaking at that, has been heavily at the expense of reading as the art of thought-getting and thought manipulation....By silently reading meanings from the first day of reading, and by practice in getting meanings from the page at the naturally rapid rate at which meanings come from situations in actual life, the rate of reading and of thinking will grow with the pupil's growth and with his power to assimilate what is read. [p. 359].

Huey addressed himself to the content of the reading primers of his day:

> Next to the beauty of the primers, the most striking thing about at least three-fourths of them is the inanity and disjointedness of their reading content, especially in the earlier parts. No trouble has been taken to write what the child would naturally say about the subject in hand, nor indeed, usually, to say *anything* connectedly and continuously as even an adult would naturally talk about the subject. The language used often shows a patronizing attempt to 'get down to the child's level', and results in a mongrel combination of points of view and of expression that is natural neither to an adult nor to a child...[pp. 278–279].

Huey provided some sentences from primers that were in common use in 1907 and were "highly recommended": "Is this a ball? Is an apple round? I can do many things. You see my dog? Run, little squirrel, run. Can you see the rat? It is a fat rat. Does the cat see the rat?" Huey claimed that: "...The primers contain hundreds of just such sentences, and yet one of the authors insists that all reading should be 'like talking.' How a child could talk such stuff naturally is beyond comprehension...[p. 280]."

A quick perusal of a reader in use in the first grade today (Clymer & Barrett, 1979) indicates that not much has changed in this regard in over ¾ of a century. Early in this more recent reader we find such natural, flowing prose as: "Here is Bill. Here is Ben. Ben said, 'No, Lad, no.' Bill said, 'No,

Jill, No.' Jill and Bill are here. Ben is here. Is Lad here? [Clymer & Barrett, 1979, pp. 11–13]."

By the end of the reader the prose has progressed to: "Jill said, 'Look at Ben!' Rosa said, 'Can we stop Ben? Ben! Stop! Stop and look! [pp. 43–45]."

Huey's comments about early primers appear to be as apt now as they were in 1908:

> The early lessons are apt to be composed of sentences thrown together with little more than this of relation between them. Now the child, on the other hand, loves a story, loves to get somewhither in what is said, wants an outcome to the discussion, and has a persistence and continuity of thought that are constantly violated by such 'sentence hash'. Better a thousand times that we had no primers than that we inflict such travesties on the child [p. 280].

Speaking then, and for now, of the "...utter triviality of the contents of our school primers and first readers", John Dewey suggests "taking up the first half dozen such books you meet and asking yourself 'how much there is in the ideas presented worthy of respect for any intelligent child of six years [p. 305]." I hope, for the sake of Japanese and Chinese children, that the prose they experience initially is not "sentence hash." Unfortunately, according to Professor Hatano in this volume, a similar problem may exist in Japanese primers. Perhaps Chinese primers are less insidious.

(5.) What about parents? Harold's data indicate that Chinese children spend more time on their homework. These data suggest that Chinese mothers provide their children with more direct help with homework, provide extra-school lessons and tutoring, attempt to minimize chores at home and, it appears, support and inculcate in their children a great respect for teachers. For these parents, school apparently is uniformly considered "real business".

Much of this is laudable and certainly contrasts with the attitudes of many American parents. But there are tradeoffs involved here that American parents, for the most part, don't seem ready to make (or at least, their willingness to make such tradeoffs appears more variable). American parents may *not* be ready to accept fully the proposition that, from the beginning, school is "real business". Spending two hours a day with their children on homework and doing more of the "housework" would be difficult in view of the increasing trend that has more and more mothers working full or parttime, out of the home. Extra-school lessons and tutoring, which appear to give Chinese children a competitive edge, are expensive and may be perceived as putting too big a strain on the family budget. Many American parents believe deeply that having their child perform regular chores is part and parcel of socialization and training for later independence. American parents are reluctant to grant teachers the independence and total support and respect accorded teachers in

Chinese culture. I'm not sure just how much difference these factors make, but they probably *do* make a difference.

(6.) What about teachers? The status of teachers is very high in Taiwan. Whereas there does not seem to be a similar notion to the Japanese *sensei* (Singleton, 1972) — used both as a noun and as the honorific form of address for respected elders, medical doctors, priests, professors, and school teachers — the public status of teachers in Taiwan, as well as their salaries, are fairly high (Stevenson, personal communication, April, 1985).

Contrast the position of school teachers in contemporary American society. Even as early as 1835, it was recognized that high standards would not be met, nor professional teachers secured, until salaries increased sufficiently to attract and hold competent persons in teaching (Butts & Cremin, 1953). Orville Taylor (1835) was direct and clear in arguing that only as the well-qualified teachers — whom higher salaries would attract — were employed, would the utility and "character" of schools be brought to an adequate standard. What Taylor said in 1835 seems equally valid in 1985: "*There is no employment among the American people...which receives less pay than elementary teaching.* Yes, there is no service so menial, no drudgery so degrading, which does not demand as high wages as we are now giving for that which is the life of our liberty, and the guard of our free institutions [p. 115]". Butts and Cremin (1953) give some historical perspective on the low status and pay of elementary school teachers:

> In a society with as strong an emphasis on individual economic success as nineteenth century America, it is not difficult to see how low economic remuneration would go hand in hand with low social status. Once again, a number of factors combined to keep the teacher from occupying a place of great respect in the community....One was the youth of teachers in general; the other was their rapid turnover. For many persons teaching was a temporary stop-gap job until marriage, business, or some other more permanent career was possible. More than anything else, perhaps, the inferior social status of the American teacher during these years was reflected in stereotypes which began to develop. The best known of these was Washington Irving's character Ichabod Crane. Here was an eccentric, ugly old man, sour, tempestuous, and unable to succeed in anything except teaching. On the female side, in spite of the youth of teachers, they were pictured as prim spinsters-to-be, entirely unapproachable by any ordinary human male. It is not difficult to see how many shied away from teaching as a permanent career [p. 285].

Although the picture for the profession of teaching in America is less grim than it was at the turn of the century, it is certainly fair to conclude that Taiwanese (and Japanese) teachers are relatively higher paid and have significantly more status than their American counterparts. In a major sense, the culture sees to this. Chinese culture seems to set things up so that discipline is not a major issue for teachers (i.e., cross the teacher, and parents will come down on you like a ton of bricks). Moral education, socialization, civility, and citizenship are engendered at home, rather than being left to the school.

(7.) What about the culture of schooling? In Taiwan, as in Japan (Singleton, 1972), teachers stress and encourage cooperation rather than competition in school. Further, homogeneity rather than heterogeneity of performance is stressed. The curriculum is uniform, and teachers appear to treat children uniformly. Emphasis seems to be getting all children to a certain performance level, with the faster students expected to "bootstrap" their slower peers. (Is this possibly an explanation for the lower reported rates of reading disabilities in China, i.e., children with reading disabilities don't get selected out).

In contrast, American schooling — a reflection of American cultural values — stresses diversity rather than homogeneity and competition (i.e., individualism) more than cooperation, and selection is not made solely (or largely) on the basis of national examinations. We, in effect use round-robin reading as a selection and management device. We have selective promotion and retention. We "track" children. From elementary school on, we have "magnet" schools, admission to which is selective and based on IQ, early achievement scores, and teacher recommendation. The culture of schooling in America is extremely number-conscious.

The Tyranny of Numbers. Or, What's Convincing us that America is Failing its Children and its Future?

Both the Chinese and the American cultures are test oriented, but in different ways. Achievement tests in Taiwan appear to be used as selection devices for admission into secondary schools. Exams are used as a social selection device for both high school and the pecking order of the prestigious universities.

Henry Steele Commager (1950) characterized Americans in the 1890s as having a "quantitative cast of mind". They measured "worth" in numbers — How big? How much? How many? Things haven't changed in that regard since the 1890s. Achievement tests were originally designed, by Edward L. Thorndike among others, to be used as an aggregate indicator to compare the performance of schools, not children. In America we use achievement (and other tests) to keep score. An individual's achievement score is much like a person's salary or the number of missiles in our national arsenal. Achievement test performances

— are presumed to be a quantitative rendering of the child's status for purposes of placement and accountability.

— are taken as a barometer of the state of morality and as a measure of success/failure of the American Democratic Experiment (Commager, 1950; Siegel & White, 1982).

—are, in the aggregate, the basis for allocation and reallocation of resources.

We use scores to pose impossible—but ponderable—calculational questions, e.g., If Jeffrey has learned to read at grade level with an overall school budget set at $1000 per child, how much will we increase Jeffrey's reading level if we increase the budget by $300 per year per child?

Reading Achievement in the Context of Society: Cultural Constraints

The United States is a relatively affluent society, and it is a pluralistic society. We pride ourselves in diversity (which we have historically done), and we ask that our schools accomplish multiple goals. We have some deep-felt belief that our schools should teach our children: (1) academic skills—the conceptual forms of a modern society (White & White, 1980); (2) citizenship—the social forms of a modern society; (3) aesthetic skills, e.g., art and music; (4) manual and technical skills; (5) physical skills—typically expressed in sports competition; (6) something like "cathexis," or love for learning for its own sake; (7) an attitude that "winning"—coming in first—is important. How big a price are we willing to pay—i.e., how much of (4), (5), (6), and (7) is American society prepared to sacrifice to emulate the Chinese (or Japanese) for slightly higher achievement scores?

Lee et al. provide suggestive data that even though our children may be doing less well in academic skills, American parents are less dissatisfied than their Chinese counterparts with the job schools are doing. Could that be due, in part, to American parents' thinking differently about what schools should be expected to do? Given those complex expectations, maybe the schools aren't really doing that bad a job. Why do lower numbers bother us? Do lower numbers mean that we really will lose our technological edge?

The Chinese and Japanese depend for economic success on sheer numbers of children achieving beyond a certain point on the distribution of academic and technical skills. America has historically not relied on a large number of "competent" people, but on a small number of "super-creative" people—many of whom didn't get along with the traditional curriculum.

The general and special theory of relativity was proposed by a relatively unschooled postal clerk. The telephone was invented by a mechanically clever dropout. The Polaroid camera process was invented by a dyslexic. Can we afford *not* to include more than the "basics" in the curriculum? Would our society be better off without manually and artistically gifted people and the experiences they might have in schools with a diverse curriculum?

I'm not trying to push the American model of education as the "one best system" (Tyack, 1974), nor am I trying to downplay many of the positive features of the Chinese educational system. It's not simply a matter of which is "better." Given the systematic differences, a more reasonable question to ask might be, "what can we sensibly borrow?" We're not borrowing just strategies, tactics, and techniques to improve reading or math scores — we're borrowing tradeoffs. In short, I am simply trying to point out that different educational systems have different adaptive value in different cultures — it's more than simply learning to read that operates under cultural constraints.

REFERENCES

Butts, R. F., & Cremin, L. A. (1953). *History of education in America.* New York: Henry Holt & Co.

Clymer, T., & Barrett, C. C. (1979). *On our way.* Lexington, MA: Ginn.

Commager, H. S. (1950). *The American mind: An interpretation of American thought and character since the 1890s.* New Haven: Yale University Press.

Huey, E. B. (1908). *The psychology and pedagogy of reading.* New York: MacMillan.

Papert, S. (1980). *Mindstorms: Children, computers, and powerful ideas.* New York: Basic Books.

Resnick, D. P., & Resnick, L. B. (1977). The nature of literacy: An historical exploration. *Harvard Educational Review, 47,* 370–385.

Siegel, A. W. (1981). The externalization of cognitive maps by children and adults: In search of ways to ask better questions. In L. S. Liben, A. Patterson, & N. Newcombe (Eds.), *Spatial representation and behavior across the life span: Theory and application.* New York: Academic Press, pp. 167–194.

Siegel, A. W., & White, S. H. (1982). The child-study movement: Early growth and development of the symbolized child. In H. W. Reese (Ed.), *Advances in Child Development and Behavior* (Vol. 17). New York: Academic Press, pp. 233–285.

Singleton, J. (1972). *Nichu: A Japanese school.* New York: Holt, Rinehart, & Winston.

Stevenson, H. W., Lee, S., Stigler, J., Kitamura, S., Kitamura, T., & Tadahisa, T. (in press). Achievement in mathematics. In H. Azuma, K. Hakuta, & H. W. Stevenson (Eds.), *Kodomo: Child development and education in Japan.* San Francisco: Freeman.

Stevenson, H. W., Lee, S., Stigler, J., Kitamura, S., & Hsu, S. (in press). Reading Japanese. In H. Azuma, K. Hakuta, & H. W. Stevenson (Eds.), *Komodo: Child development and education in Japan.* San Francisco: Freeman.

Taylor, J. O. (1835). *The district school; or, National education.* Philadelphia: Carey, Lea, & Blanchard.

Tyack, D. B. (1974). *The one best system: A history of American urban education.* Cambridge, MA: Harvard University Press.

White, S. H. (1978). Psychology in all sorts of places. In R. A. Kasschau & F. S. Kessel (Eds.), *Houston Symposium I. Psychology and society: In search of symbiosis.* New York: Holt, Rinehart, & Winston, pp. 105–131.

White, S. H., & White, B. N. (1980). *Childhood: Pathways of discovery.* Holland: Multimedia Publications Inc.

White, S. H., & Siegel, A. W. (1984). Cognitive development time and space. In B. Rogoff & J. Lave (Eds.). *Everyday cognition: Its development in social context.* Cambridge MA: Harvard University Press, pp. 238–277.

Author Index

Subject Index